Question-Driven Data Projects

Optimizing Business Value with the
Right Questions

Zacharias Voulgaris, PhD

Technics Publications

115 Linda Vista, Sedona, AZ 86336 USA
https://www.TechnicsPub.com

Cover design by Lorena Molinari
Edited by Jamie Hoberman

First Edition

First Printing 2024

Copyright © 2024 Zacharias Voulgaris, PhD

ISBN, print ed.   9781634625180
ISBN, Kindle ed.   9781634625227
ISBN, PDF ed.   9781634625234

Library of Congress Control Number: 2024943644

To Laura and Przemek

Contents

PART I

Can we focus on the data at hand for a moment?

"What a wonderful thing it would be if all our questions were answered!"

J.M. Barrie (Peter Pan)

What if we have been going about data the wrong way?

"Asking the right question is more than half the battle of finding the (right) answer."

Thomas J. Watson

We are immersed in an ocean of data yet dying of thirst. This seems like a paradox, but it is a great metaphor for our situation, where there is an abundance of data, most of which we cannot leverage. Just like not all water is good for us to drink, we can't process any kind of data that comes our way. The data professionals are sometimes to blame, but not always. Sometimes we approach the problem in a nonconstructive manner. If we leaders fail to envision and pursue a solution, how can we expect a knowledge worker to succeed (even if that person better understands the data at hand)?

Back to the water example, although most ocean water is useless for human consumption, some people have managed to overcome this issue. The Canary Islands, for example, have a working solution to this problem even though they don't have a lot of resources available. Yet, they have developed a significant desalination capacity (about 2% of the global capacity, which is impressive considering that the population of that part of the world is a bit less than 0.03%

of the global population). So, perhaps we, too, can overcome the ocean of data challenges we face, regardless of where we are.

There is little doubt that the data pipeline framework is mature these days. Even newcomers in the field can tell you how to build a data product, whether that's a dashboard, a predictive model, or some more complex system. They may also provide you with a bunch of insights, many of which are interesting. But often, we find out that this work doesn't deliver the value you have come to expect. It seems to be fine when you look at it closely, but when it comes to the value it's supposed to deliver, it leaves much to desire. Could it be that somehow you were led astray?

Before we start pointing fingers, it's best to take a step back. Maybe it wasn't the data workers' fault after all. This doesn't mean it was your fault as a decision-maker, either. Could the whole matter be more convoluted than it first seemed?

One of the things you learn working in the start-up world is that there are no failures, just lessons. If we adopt this approach in the whole data process gone wrong, perhaps we can learn something to help us fix things or at least fix the projects at hand. Then, we can apply what we learned and iterate, noting the improvements in the result.

It may sound generic as advice, but this doesn't make it inapplicable. So, instead of discarding it as something we already "know," it would be best to look into it and see how we can apply it to the problem(s) at hand. One great way to do that is by asking questions.

When Tomas Watson said, "Asking the right question is more than half the battle of finding the (right) answer," he was definitely on to something. After all, he was the CEO of one of the world's most prominent computer companies that later started dabbling in AI (IBM). If the name sounds familiar, it's because one of the first real-world AI systems, IBM's Watson, was named after him (even if many people may believe that it was related to Arthur Conan Doyle's sidekick character, John Watson!).

Asking the right questions is something that many people may have opted for since antiquity. This endeavor was more philosophical, though philosophy and science weren't that clearly defined back then. Many prominent philosophers were knowledgeable in Math and Astronomy, popular scientific fields at the time. Data may not have been a relevant term at the time. Still, many more practical people started applying this philosophical approach to solve real-world problems or at least gain a solid understanding of the world through a more scientific approach to the topics at hand.

Data and science are intertwined, even when the former has been relatively scarce in previous eras. This more data-driven approach to finding answers has been very popular throughout history, particularly in Western civilization. When Kepler came up with his famous laws about the movement of celestial bodies, he didn't pick them out of a hat. He worked with data collected via astronomical observations over many years. Then, with a lot of strenuous work, he summarized the gist of this data through a series of mathematical equations. These were among the first data models in science, and it is believed that they may have helped Newton with his work on the Theory of Gravity.

Although the data-driven process is powerful, its strength derives primarily from the (right) questions people leading it ask and try to answer. That's something many people tend to forget today as their reliance on existing data models, heuristics, and various other methods robs them of the depth and often also the breadth of their investigations. This also leads to decisions of a lesser quality, inevitably.

It's not that the existing models and heuristics are inherently bad—our over-reliance on them is the problem.

After all, these are all tools and accessories, not substitutes for our reasoning, decision making, and strategizing about the problems we deal with. Perhaps that's why AI systems haven't delivered on their creators' promises yet; they can do a lot of the heavy lifting for us, but they cannot take us by the hand and solve all our problems, at least not in a way that benefits us holistically.

To make this more concrete, let's look at the problem of getting from A to B using a car. A data model may help us find the optimal route to get there in the least amount of time, or with the least expensive way, or maybe through a combination of factors. However, we still need to decide on the route and get there! Even the much-promising self-driving cars may fall short of taking us there in a way that's 100% problem-free.

Problems an organization faces may seem different and even simpler, but they are not. The more long-term the strategies involved, the more complex the problems. This is especially the case when the environment (market) changes over time, sometimes significantly. Fortunately, cars don't have to deal with such drastic changes in their environment, even if the weather conditions change throughout a trip.

Data systems, particularly AI-based ones, have become adept at answering various questions. However, someone still needs to ask those questions and ask them intelligently. Some people receive a lot of money to ask you questions to get to the bottom of the problems that rob you of serenity. This makes both them and their questions valuable, especially when it comes to the skill of asking these questions and pursuing answers methodically and efficiently without losing sight of the bigger picture. Someone may argue that AI can do that, too. However, this doesn't make this skill and those practicing it less valuable. Similar to the image-generating AI system that hasn't made (good) artists obsolete.

Going back to the original scenario, let's revise our approach. Instead of blaming the data professionals, the data, or yourself, you can start exploring the matter, much like an observer would, formulating relevant questions and pursuing them. Then, once you have gathered satisfactory answers, you can start putting this information into action and steering the data project(s) accordingly. And that's where the journey (and the fun) begins!

This book attempts to get you to a place of inquisitive learning, getting deep into the subject of data. Without getting too technical, it illustrates the various aspects of the subject, focusing on their relationship to business. After all, data is supposed to be a value-add, an asset of sorts. However, many data experts these days conclude that data by itself is not of any inherent value (!) and that unless treated properly, it can end up on the other side of the spectrum: a liability. In this book, we'll explore how you can avoid that pitfall and navigate the turbulent landscape of the data-riddled world we live in today, viewing data as an opportunity for growth rather than a threat or hazard to your enterprise.

The book is structured as follows. Three main parts take you through the data journey every organization goes through in one way or another (not always in that order, however). We start with the data at hand, which is the data you already have or have easy access to. This is more or less your comfort zone and a risk-free place to explore various low-hanging fruits that can add value without breaking the bank. This part begins with examining your needs regarding the data, surveying the data you already have and the skill sets you have access to, and then zeroing in on what you can learn about the past, present, and future related to the data at hand.

In the part that follows, we view the bigger picture of data, namely the various data matters related to strategy and the data that goes beyond what you have. This is where data becomes more interesting as it's not just a resource but also a potential investment and a culture-changing force for your organization. This part includes chapters examining topics like how your data needs evolve, other data sources, additional technologies and professionals you may need, the cost of all this, and some Strengths, Weaknesses, Opportunities, and Threats (SWOT) analysis to put everything into perspective.

Finally, the last part of the book looks into artificial intelligence. Insulating you from the hype, it breaks this new tech down into bits that are easier to understand and appreciate. Namely, the chapters in this part explore how AI is involved in data work, when it would be applicable, where you can find competent AI professionals and the various kinds of information (and data) AI can handle, and whether AI is worth it as an investment for you.

Each chapter of the book tackles a particular question related to the topic. Ideally, you'd ponder on this question on your own before delving into the chapter and exploring the suggested answers and follow-up questions posed by the author. Hopefully, this will not only help you link this information with your own thoughts and knowledge but also help cultivate a sense of curiosity about the topic. Appendices will cover a series of typical questions and a proposed workflow for tackling a question. This way, after reading this book, you will better understand how to explore and go deeper on data on your own instead of relying on it as a walking aid, or, even worse, forget about it altogether!

There is no set way for making the most of this book. Maybe you discover that certain chapters contain already known information or that other chapters are more relevant to your journey and your organization's needs. Explore how you can apply the stuff covered here and cultivate a sense of data savviness. It's perfectly ok if you end up with more questions afterward. Fortunately, answers are abundant, many of which closely link to our questions. Those questions, however, are key as they will help us better integrate those answers and turn this information into knowledge and beyond. This is the quintessence of data work and those of us who have participated in it view it as insightful and valuable. Perhaps you partake in this endeavor too, turning data into value and an asset.

Are you ready to take the first steps?

ONE

What do you need from the data?

"It's better to know some of the questions than all of the answers."

James Thurber

1.1 What does this mean, exactly?

Different people have different needs; organizations aren't any different in that respect. What you or your organization needs may not be the same as what your competitor needs (though there is bound to be some overlap). Therefore, blindly imitating their actions when it comes to data work isn't going to yield any long-term benefits. It's great that you are aware of the fact, but how is it best to leverage that?

Every organization has certain needs to optimize its revenue streams, minimize risk, and maximize customer experience. Perhaps the first point isn't relevant if yours is a not-for-profit, but it doesn't hurt to have it in mind. Regardless of your organization's profile, chances are that you already need something from the data at hand and may already have done something about it. Just like a street vendor uses microeconomics, even if they have no concept of what the field entails, you may be leveraging data already in some modality.

However, not all businesses need a link to data. Sometimes, it's just good old-fashioned business processes that come into play. Other times, just that personal touch helps you win customers and foster long-term relationships with them. And in some situations, it's just that innate feeling you have, that intuition, if you will, that prompts you to make the right decision.

Understanding what you need from data is about figuring out how to tackle certain processes or issues you face using data analytics. Then why do we focus on data, you may wonder. Well, data analytics will not yield any fruit without data of a certain standard, which involves the right amount, quality, governance, and processing. When done in an organized and efficient manner, all this can yield insights and useful predictions (*actionable information* or even *knowledge*). All these information-like entities, including data, form a hierarchy and are known as the Data Information Knowledge Wisdom (DIKW) Pyramid (Figure 1.1).

This chapter will explore how your organization can transform data and information to meet its needs.

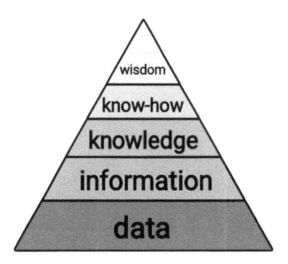

Figure 1.1: The DIKW Pyramid. Higher levels refer to more refined and/or actionable information. The "know-how" part is not always included in this model, but it's a useful addition. Note that some people refer to that level of the pyramid as "understanding." In any case, it's very important.

1.2 What are your main pain points?

When you go to a physician about an ailment, it's often the case that they start with questions about where it hurts. After all, you don't visit them and spend lots of money just to admire their white coat! The same goes when you engage in data work with a consultant or a mentor. The first and most important things we need to know about you and your organization are your key pain points. Then, we can look into how we can tackle them through data work, usually prioritizing the most urgent and important ones.

Typical pain points include excessive costs in a particular process, too much time spent in customer acquisition, ineffective marketing campaigns, understanding how the next version of a product (or service) needs to be improved, and prioritizing or developing products.

It's possible that you may have many pain points (definitely beyond this short list) and be unclear as to what to tackle first. It's often the case that you neglect the ones that are not urgent but are still important. These are important for long-term benefits and when left unattended, chances are that they will become urgent, too, eventually. These are also pain points that can be tackled with data work, at least via Proof of Concept (PoC) projects, unless you become certain that data work can deliver benefits regarding them.

In any case, this primary surveying of pain points and their classification (organizing them by urgency and importance) is something that you are better suited to do. Once you are clear about them, you can start looking into how you can leverage data to resolve them, with or without help from an external data professional.

Figure 1.2 shows a concise taxonomy of an organization's key pain points and how they may relate to data. This is not a comprehensive list, but it may help you organize your organization's various pain points and tackle them more efficiently.

Figure 1.2: Business pain point types (areas) where data can make a difference as a value-add.

1.3 What are your objectives?

Aims and objectives are paramount in business strategy and are often closely linked to data work. They also link to the pain points discussed previously. After all, pain points are the obstacles that inhibit the realization of the organization's aims. There is an old Native American Indian saying: *The obstacle is the path*. So, in a way, by tackling these pain points *with a clear aim or objective in mind*, you progress as an organization. This is why they can be viewed as a blessing in disguise, since these pain points organically divert our attention to the things that require it, those issues you need to address first. Otherwise, you may be allocating resources to other, less pressing matters.

Sometimes, pain points come about in ways that clash with our plans. We may have a security breach and lots of customer data gets compromised, even if cybersecurity wasn't part of this year's aims. This may be hurtful and a real hazard to the organization's reputation, but it's also a sign that perhaps we should have looked into this matter so that this breach wouldn't have occurred. After all, hackers tend to be highly opportunistic, so if they find that your organization's cybersecurity is tough, they'll likely go for other, easier targets. The point here is that even if the pain points (in this case, the relatively weak cybersecurity) are not aligned with your objectives, this misalignment is bound to be temporary. Chances are that once the security issues have been raised in a meeting, cybersecurity will become an objective very soon and perhaps even part of the aims of the IT department.

Ideally, you wouldn't have to change your aims and objectives in a reactive way, letting pain points dictate what you should do and when. For less random-like events, it's possible to prevent the corresponding pain points by foreseeing potential issues beforehand. That's one of the reasons why data work is important, as it enables us to do just that. For this to happen, however, we need to make sure that it's part of the aims and objectives of the organization.

1.4 How does data fit into your overall strategy?

The organization's overall strategy may not be something you have full control of, but it doesn't hurt knowing where data fits. This way, at the very least, you can advocate for its inclusion and the development of data strategy initiatives that can further data-related objectives to tackle specific pain points. Whole books and courses have been developed on data strategy and it's easy to get carried away with this topic. However, it is a relevant contact point that's worth exploring further.

A common misconception about data work and the strategy that keeps it organized and effective is that it has to do with the data at hand. However, as

Bernard Marr (an expert in this field) says, data strategy is "NOT determined by what data we have readily available but what our business wants to achieve and how data can help us get there." In other words, the business strategy expresses itself as a data strategy, too (at least in part), and the data follows. This enables the business to become more data-driven and build data pipelines around its business cases instead of the other way around. Also, Mr. Marr argues that a data-driven strategy doesn't require a very large budget, at least as a starting point.

Returning to the overall strategy, data can be a valuable asset as it can tackle specific problems and offer sustainable solutions (not necessarily in the ecological sense, but always in a way that benefits the bottom line). However, any data initiative should start from the top tiers of the organization's echelons rather than from some pet project of a data team to be successful in the long term. There is nothing wrong with grassroots initiatives in an organization regarding data. However, they won't go far without some support from management (especially from top management). An insightful leader is bound to take notice of and foster such initiatives, leveraging them as proof-of-concepts for other, more long-term projects that tackle issues of a larger scope. An even more insightful leader is bound to inspire such initiatives before they come about on their own, coordinating different teams to pursue them as part of the organization's overall strategy. We'll talk more about data strategy in Part 2 of the book. If you wish to delve deeper into data strategy, Bernard Marr's book[1] is a good place to start.

1.5 What does a successful data product look like to you?

Data work, at least the type that is of a certain scope and performed by serious data professionals, usually involves the development of some data product. The latter is any kind of product that you can use as a value-add for a specific set of customers. These can be either internal (e.g., C-level executives) or external (e.g.,

---

[1] Bernard Marr, *Data Strategy*, Kogan Page publications, October 2021.

the visitors of your organization's website). In any case, the data product is usually a stand-alone piece of software that, more often than not, takes the form of a dashboard or an API.[2]

Dashboards are essentially a number of plots and diagrams meshed together to provide the user with an accurate picture of a situation. Sometimes, they are even dynamic, particularly when the data changes in real time. Although there is an element of aesthetics in dashboards, that's not the most important thing. First and foremost, relevant information needs to be presented in them, not just any graphic that looks good. Ideally, the plots in a dashboard would convey key insights that will help decision making and drive action. Bernard Marr puts it more succinctly like this: "If the key insights aren't clearly presented, they won't result in action."

What about you? What do you expect from a dashboard? Think of a specific example of a dashboard you would need to aid your decisions. Can you describe it as a set of points (requirements)? If so, you are ready to talk to a data professional and assign them that task. Naturally, you may need to have some iterations until you are both on the same page. This iterative process is much easier today as many of these dashboards are created programmatically and are not too time-consuming in their editing.

APIs are how the users experience various data models in practice. They involve a substantial amount of coding, though some of it may be already there as a

---

[2] API stands for *Application Programming Interface* and refers to a piece of code that enables two computers to talk to each other and exchange data. Usually one of them requests something and the other processes that request and responds to it. APIs are commonly used today, especially in web-based applications. Whenever you get a map on a business website showing you the location of their venue, chances are that some map-related API is working behind the scenes.

template, so it doesn't require a huge amount of time, especially if the data professional or developer knows what they are doing. An example of an API that may be useful to a bank employee, for example, would be one that takes some key data from the user (the banker) regarding a potential client (e.g., someone who needs a mortgage) and yields whether that person should receive that loan and (ideally) the most important reasons why. The API might also suggest a fair interest rate, given the risk of default from the particular customer based on the data model behind the scenes.

What would a good API look like for you? Consider a particular use case where you would need some information (not just data) to decide based on available data. What kind of data would you need to exchange with this API? If you have a clear idea and access to the relevant data, you have taken the first and most important step towards developing an API to solve a particular problem for your organization. Naturally, this may take some time to happen. The API technology may be straightforward, but the data model behind the scenes still needs time to build, test, and deploy.

1.6 Would any of this be possible without data analytics?

It's doubtful that any of this would be possible without data analytics, particularly the kind under the data science umbrella. Maybe a few decades ago, you could get by with some basic analytics, often conducted in a spreadsheet application and some database, but things have evolved a lot since then. It's not that these technologies are not relevant anymore. However, to get any kind of business advantage these days, you need to take it up a notch or two. One of the ways to accomplish this is via data analytics, which often incorporates some AI-based models. Speaking of AI, that's another way to add value on the data side. However, this deserves its own set of chapters, so if you are eager to explore that, you may want to jump to Chapter 11 (not the scary one!).

But what is data analytics? Surely, it involves more than crunching numbers with some stats formulas and using the advanced settings on a calculator! Data analytics is a vast field involving various methods that ingest, process, and analyze data, presenting the insights and predictions that come about during the process. In one of my previous books,[3] the whole field is explored in depth without getting too technical. Some would argue that data analytics is a broader field than data science, yet the two terms are interchangeable today. After all, many a data analyst will eventually become a data scientist if they continue progressing in their career. Nevertheless, as a data analyst is often more affordable for an organization, the role is bound to persist in the foreseeable future.

In practice, a team of professionals conducts data analytics (especially the more advanced kind). Such a team may consist of a variety of roles, for example, a data scientist, a data engineer, a data visualization specialist, a data analyst, an AI expert, and a data storyteller. It's unlikely that a team would have all of these roles, especially in the beginning, but it's possible to have many different combinations, depending on the project at hand. The people in those roles may work on different projects, often at the same time, and be allocated based on what is needed. How, where, when, and what is done by whom is usually dictated by the organization's data strategy and the pain points these projects aim to tackle. Once viewed from this perspective, everything starts falling into place. The key thing is to be clear about the objectives of these projects and how they align with the organization's specific needs, as well as to have responsible individuals in key positions driving these projects. That's something that all the data in the world can't replace (at least not yet)!

---

[3] Zacharias Voulgaris, *Data Science: Mindset, Methodologies, and Misconceptions*, Technics Publications, 2017.

1.7 Key takeaways

- **Understand your organization's unique needs**: Recognize that every organization has different needs, goals, and challenges.

- **Focus on data analytics to address specific pain points**: Identify the processes or issues that can be improved using data analytics.

- **Identify key pain points and organize them**: When starting a data project, it's essential to identify your organization's most critical pain points. Organize them into categories based on urgency and importance.

- **Aims and objectives drive business strategy**: Clear aims and objectives are crucial in business strategy, and they're closely linked to data work.

- **Data strategy links to business strategy**: Data strategy shouldn't be determined by available data but rather by what the business wants to achieve and how data can help achieve those goals.

- **Top-down support crucial for long-term success**: While grassroots initiatives are fine, they may not go far without top management support.

- **Data work involves developing data products**: Data professionals typically develop stand-alone software products that provide value-add for specific customers (e.g., executives or website visitors).

- **Dashboards and APIs are types of data products**: Dashboards present relevant information clearly and concisely, while APIs provide access to specific data models through programming interfaces.

- **Data analytics is crucial for business advantage**: In today's digital age, to gain a competitive edge, organizations need to leverage advanced data analytics techniques, often incorporating AI-based models.

What data do you have?

2.1 What does data entail, exactly?

Data is a ubiquitous term that covers a large variety of things. As we saw in the previous chapter, it's at the base of the DIKW pyramid and constitutes the basis of any meaningful data project. Often, we express information or even knowledge as data, too. So, in practice, it's an umbrella term that covers all kinds of information that can be processed, analyzed, and transformed into something insightful or actionable. Examples of data in a typical business include customer data (e.g., demographics, ratings, etc.), financial data, operational data, sales and revenue data, marketing and advertising data, human resources data, and market research data. Even if you don't leverage a lot of this data, it's still there and easily accessible to you and (hopefully) the analysts. An overview of the various kinds of data you can find, organized in terms of departments, can be viewed in Figure 2.1.

Fortunately, nowadays, almost everything leaves a trace or trail or data behind. Although this may not always be good news, especially for anyone who values their privacy, it makes data more widely available as a resource. So, there is no shortage of data, even if you are unaware of the various flows around you.

Figure 2.1: Areas in an organization involving data you may have access to for data projects.

As data can be very diverse and even chaotic, it is often organized in databases or various kinds and managed by people with the relevant skill sets. In its crudest form, data is useless and possibly a liability (after all, it costs to store and manage it). In an organized form, it's still without inherent value but potentially useful. But first, let's look at the different categories of data to understand it better and examine how each one can be leveraged properly.

2.2 What are the different kinds of data?

There are as many different taxonomies of data as there are types of experts! All of them are useful in their own context but not always useful when deriving value from the data at hand. In data work, particularly, there are three main types of data:

- Structured (most of the data you'll encounter)
- Unstructured (most challenging kind)
- Semi-structured

Traditionally, the first kind of data has been the bread and butter of most analysts, including data analysts. This is the kind of data you'll find in a well-maintained spreadsheet or in an old-fashioned database. Such data has an unchanging number of columns, making it easy to work with. Naturally, even querying such a collection of data is very efficient, while it's easy to combine data from various places, as long as there are logical links among those places. This is typically the most widely spread kind of data and is bound to yield value in the most accessible projects you bring to life.

Unstructured data is more chaotic and it involves data that doesn't have any kind of structure whatsoever. Typical examples of such data are texts in a natural language, computer code, and a participant's notes from a meeting. Although chances are that you will encounter mostly the first kind of unstructured data, you may ask yourself, "How is such data ever going to be useful?" and you would be right. After all, you are not running a literature convention or a library. However, natural language has become increasingly popular, appearing in surveys, customer reviews, and other places where you get feedback about your products or services. Modern AI thrives with this kind of data, although there are also more traditional ways to process it, leveraging specialized data professionals.

The last kind of data, semi-structured, is a bit more tricky, though not uncommon. This type of data has some structure but it is not as clear-cut or well-defined as the data that lives in a table. Semi-structured data may be things like the results of a non-trivial survey (where different people answer different questions, depending on their answers), a web page (the code of a website has some structure to it, though it varies from page to page and from site to site), and most modern databases (e.g., MongoDB, knowledge graphs, etc.). Semi-structured data is not too challenging to process as we can often transform it into structured data. However, it's not as fast to process as structured data, and you may require additional resources (including specialized professionals) to process it efficiently.

How is all this important to you? Well, if you want to make the most of your various data assets, you will need to get the right people working on it. Before hiring or spending money on consultants, survey your organization and see what kinds of data you have. This will enable you to ask better questions afterward.

2.3 Where can you look for the data you have?

Good quality data is sometimes like the value in crypto-currencies: highly elusive. However, if you search for it and gather enough of it, you may find what you are looking for without having to spend any money or take any unnecessary risks.

The first place to search for data is within your databases. Surveying the tables in these databases and gathering the architectural diagrams are good places to start. After all, you don't need to know the specific records in those databases, just the kind of variables that are stored and how they are connected. Start with a data architect if you have one. Otherwise, track down the database administrators.

Naturally, not every piece of data will be as neatly organized as the data you find in a database. However, this doesn't mean that you should stop there. You can also find invaluable data in other places, such as spreadsheets. These may not always lend themselves to efficient data processing, but they are great as a source of data. Although spreadsheets don't have the neat form of a database table, you can access them with a programming language and get all the data without anyone having to do anything in your spreadsheet application (e.g., Excel). Naturally, you may need to note the permissions required for someone to access the part of the organization's computer network and ensure your analysts have that.

Web forms are another source of useful data in an organization. These usually link to specific databases. These web forms are also a way to interface with potential customers, so getting hold of that data and analyzing it is significant. You can also easily create new forms for the organization's website and use them for specific data projects. Alternatively, you can use third-party form software, like Google Forms, to gather data from the people you are interested in.

Beyond these places, other ones are more organization-specific. For example, if you do lots of surveys or polls, you may accumulate lots of data from them. These can be very valuable in getting to know your customers or leads. Additionally, combined with other data points from the aforementioned sources, this data can be more information-rich and yield insights you may not have gathered otherwise. After all, data has a synergy effect, so gathering a lot of it and a large variety of it has its advantages.

2.4 How much can be harnessed in a data project?

That's a much better question than it first seems. After all, we face a lot of misleading information about data and how big data can solve all of our problems. However, the reality of it is that often, less is more. That's particularly the case with most data, as most data does not exist for the purpose of a data product or even a data project, for that matter.

The short answer to the question is lots of it, but not all. How much exactly will depend on the problem you are trying to solve and the models involved. If it's a complex problem that doesn't have an easy solution, you may need to break it down into smaller and simpler problems and solve each separately. For instance, say that your organization doesn't get much engagement from its website's visitors. That's a problem that can be tackled with data, but it's not a trivial one. You may want to break it down into the following problems:

- What are these visitors like?
- Where do they spend the most time when browsing our site?
- Could a different design (e.g., a bigger button for the call-to-action) make a difference?
- What about a different color palette?

- Which of these visitors end up contacting us or making an order?

Each one of these mini problems may be manageable on its own or it may need further decomposition. For example, the "different design" one lends itself to many different interpretations if we don't limit its scope. Ideally, we'd explore three to five of the most promising designs (which should be simple to implement through alternative CSS files or via a different plug-in, depending on the kind of site). Then, analyze how each one performs through a series of A-B tests. It has become a more manageable and quantifiable problem we can easily solve once we gather data from the website's server.

The models used are also an important factor. More complex models, such as the ones commonly used today (e.g., AI models), need more data. Also, they tend to do their own pre-processing of that data, so if you feed them extra variables, they can discern whether they should use them. You may need significantly less data for simpler models (e.g., a decision tree or a bunch of such trees in an ensemble formation). Naturally, different models may have different levels of performance. Still, it's important to remember that if you don't have tons of data, a more complex model may not be able to deliver an edge to justify its computational cost.

What models you use are closely linked to the people you leverage for this task. An entry-level professional may be more geared toward the simpler models (and there is nothing wrong with that), while more experienced or specialized professionals may gravitate toward the latest and greatest models. In any case, it's usually the data professionals' call. You should be fine if you have a knowledgeable and unbiased person to lead the analytics team. If you are that person, then you probably have skipped this section altogether!

In any case, how much data you use may not be as important as the quality of that data. It's best to focus on that as well as on how the data relates to the problem you are trying to solve. A variable that may be good for a certain data project may be utterly useless for another one. The same goes with the models, to some extent. That's why it's crucial not to delete any data but to be extra careful about what you use and where. After all, the value of the data is always very relative.

2.5 How does time come into play?

Time is an important factor in the data world, particularly if we use this data to provide actionable insights for the present and the future. Data may be great for the analysts when they dig into it first, but when it's time to deliver something of value from it, it may be that it's just not fresh enough. In other words, it is suffering from data staleness. This is the case when the information in the data is no longer relevant to the stuff it tries to reflect. It will be even worse if you plan to use that data for predictions.

This data needs to be acquired recently and reflect recent developments to be relevant to the data at hand. For example, if we have customer data on how certain individuals interact with a specific product that is no longer for sale (or has been changed significantly in its latest iterations), that data may not be useful to the organization. Fortunately, not all data suffers from this problem, since demographic data doesn't change as fast and can be used for many years without diluting the information involved. However, other kinds of data, such as transaction data, user behavior on the web, and anything that is relatively non-deterministic, are prone to staleness and lack of relevance.

When data has time stamps attached to it, it becomes even more valuable in a particular kind of analytics. The latter is called time series analysis (aka, TSA, but not the airport kind!) and it's very useful in various areas. Particularly when it comes to financial data, TSA is very important. In most cases in TSA, the variable we are trying to predict is the same as the one we use to make these predictions. Naturally, we can also have other variables in this analysis, especially if they are time stamped.

Finally, other factors may bring time into the data landscape (the datascape,[4] if you will). These may be related to the particular domain of the organization, the location (e.g., data related to weather may be quite different in countries of the other hemisphere), etc. Hopefully, all this can help you come up with other relevant questions to ask before leveraging the data at hand to make the most of it and improve its quality.

2.6 What potential value exists in your data?

We can harness data in various ways to produce value for your organization via data products and insights. However, the link between data products and business needs isn't always apparent, so be clear about what you want to accomplish with the data at hand. Is there a particular process you wish to optimize, like minimizing waste or maximizing ROI? Is there a new kind of service you wish to provide to your customers to improve their experience on your website or in your stores? The sky is the limit.

It's good to remember that no matter how high this limit is, there is always a limit to the value data can bring. If there are serious issues with the business model or large-scale problems with the organization's processes, it's doubtful data can make everything fine.

The potential of the data also greatly depends on the technologies used. You may have a plethora of data points and the quality of this data may be sublime, but the analysts tasked to work with the data may not deliver much value because of the models they are using. That's why data literacy across the organization is so

---

[4] This is a concept introduce by IBM in 2014 as part of their Internet of Things (IoT) strategy. In refers to the "digital ecosystem that combines people, data, and devices to create new experiences and insights."

important, especially for people in leadership positions. Understanding the reality of data beyond the hype entails technologies, too, though it goes beyond that.

You can think of data like the fuel of a vehicle. Without it, it won't be able to go anywhere, but even with good fuel, the vehicle still needs to be in good condition, with its engine properly maintained, the driver sober, and with some experience in driving, etc. The fuel by itself cannot and will not do much.

The most important thing that helps derive value from the data isn't the technology but the professionals involved in the data processes. This is something that deserves a chapter of its own, though. Having someone in the driver's seat in the vehicle of our example isn't enough, especially if you want to make the most of your data and arrive at your destination efficiently.

2.7 Key takeaways

- **Data is abundant and widely available**: With the increasing digitization of our world, almost everything leaves a trail of data behind it, making it readily accessible.

- **Three main types of data**: *Structured* (easy to work with, typical in databases), *Unstructured* (lacks structure, examples include texts and computer code), and *Semi-Structured* (has some structure but varies, like survey results or web pages).

- **Understanding data types is crucial for deriving value**: Knowing the type of data you have is important for determining how to process and utilize it effectively.

- **Search for good quality data within your organization's databases:** There you can find valuable information about variables and connections. If needed, consult with database administrators or data architects to access this data.

- **Good quality data is often elusive**, but gathering many data points can have a synergy effect, allowing you to uncover valuable insights without spending anything.

- **The amount of data needed to solve a problem** depends on the complexity of the problem, the models used, and the project's goals. Often, less data is more effective, especially when using simpler models like decision trees. To determine how much data you need, break down complex problems into smaller, manageable ones, and focus on collecting high-quality data that relates to the specific problem you're trying to solve.

- **"Data staleness" occurs when data is no longer relevant or fresh,** making it less useful for analysis. This can be particularly problematic if you're trying to use the data for predictions.

- **Data limitations**: It's crucial to remember that data has its limits and cannot solve all problems. If there are significant issues with the business model or organization processes, data may not be enough to fix everything.

- **Data as fuel**: Data can be thought of as the fuel that powers a vehicle. Without it, nothing can happen, but even with good fuel, the vehicle still needs to be in good condition, with proper maintenance, an experienced driver, etc.

- **Value-added insights**: The ultimate goal is to use data to generate value-added insights that drive business outcomes. This requires a combination of clear goals, high-quality data, effective analytics models, and skilled professionals involved in the data process.

THREE

What kind of skillsets are available?

"You can tell whether a man is wise by his questions."

Naguib Mahfouz

3.1 What does this question mean, exactly?

It's likely that you probably don't have all the skillsets you need to harness data end-to-end. Even if you do, you are probably better off outsourcing at least part of the work required to other people so that you can focus on big-picture matters. Having access to different skillsets enables you to do that. The people with these skillsets may not be in your organization already, but if you know what you are looking for, chances are that it won't be that difficult to find them.

An old adage says, "If you want to go somewhere in the fastest possible way, go by yourself. If you want to go the farthest, go with others." Successful data teams are rarely a one-person-team situation. So, no matter how skilled you are, you are better off getting other skilled individuals around you and tackling data projects together, harnessing the data at hand to address the pain points.

In this chapter, we'll tackle questions like what skillsets come into play, what people have such skillsets, whether you can train existing professionals for these skills, how mastery of these skills factors in, and the value of these skillsets.

3.2 What are the skillsets that come into play?

A variety of skillsets play a role in a data project, from the more obvious ones, like project management and data analysis, to less apparent ones, like data visualization and storytelling. In Figure 3.1, you can see an overview of all the skillsets found in a data project, though not all are always present in every such project. Think of these as a pool of skills clustered in various groups often associated with specific roles. The roles may have a one-to-one relationship with data professionals, or there may be data professionals that cover two or more roles, depending on the versatility of these individuals.

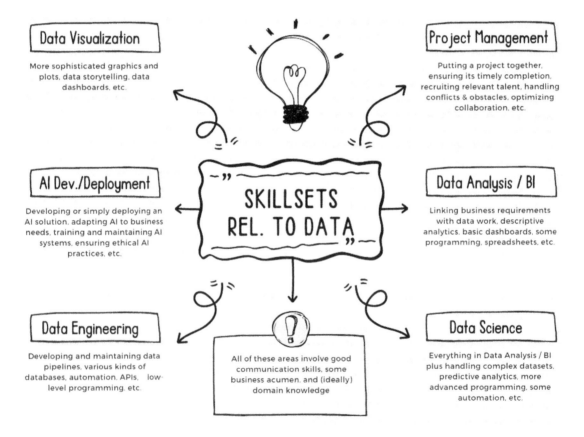

Figure 3.1: Skillsets related to data work and brief descriptions of them.

First and foremost, you need certain management skills, particularly project management. Ideally, you'd also have a program/product manager, but senior management and project managers can split the relevant skills. This is an important skillset, though, since without proper coordination and liaising with the business side of things, a data project may fail to deliver adequate value. Most data professionals tend to have a different perspective than business people and their understanding of value is also different. So, what may count as a successful data project for a data team may not be as successful for a business person. Good project management can ensure that the two perspectives are aligned and abide by the resource limitations of the organization.

Data analysis and Business Intelligence (BI) are also in the mix. This is especially the case for a proof-of-concept project or for cases requiring a more basic analysis. Naturally, these skillsets are also useful for more complex projects, but in those cases, we require an additional skillset: data science. This involves more advanced models, somewhat different methodologies, and even automation. Nowadays, it's not uncommon for someone to have skills across both these skillsets.

The data engineering skillset is also paramount in a data project, particularly a complex one. It's often the case that software developers perform this role, but data engineering involves more than development work. It's also related to databases, pipeline development, data APIs, and specialized software. Even on the server side of things, the skills of a data engineer are more specialized and geared toward cloud computing. Although some data engineers can handle data modeling, the latter is usually in the domain of data science.

An AI skillset has its own cluster of skills. This involves developing and deploying an AI solution, refining it, and providing some automation. We'll talk about AI in more detail in the third part of this book, while in Chapter 13, we'll look into how you can recruit such professionals.

A data project also requires data visualization. This goes hand-in-hand with data storytelling and it's all about dashboard design, creating catchy data-related graphics (plots, charts, and even infographics), and weaving a story around the data project. Although it usually comes at the end of the project, data visuals can also be found in the early stages when understanding the data (part of the exploratory data analysis methodology, aka EDA). Sometimes, the visuals these experts develop are the project's end product, so they tend to be refined and even self-explanatory. This often borders artwork, though the insights in those visuals are always the result of focused data analytics work.

Of course, communication, business acumen, and even domain knowledge are important skills. After all, without a common language, it's hard to get people to understand each other and work well together. That's why data professionals must have business understanding and business professionals must have data literacy. Although we like to imagine different roles and skillsets on top of each other like in a traditional pyramid, in practice, they all work together and each has the same objective, the delivery of value using data. See Figure 3.2.

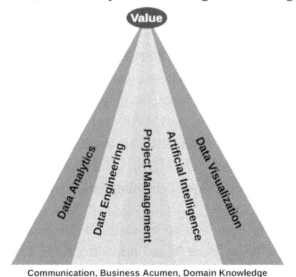

Figure 3.2: How the various skillsets fit together. Note that in this graphic data analysis and data science are merged together as Data Analytics, for the sake of simplicity.

3.3 What kind of people have such skillsets?

Now, let's look at each skillset to identify the kind of people who may possess them. This can greatly aid any hiring endeavor that may ensue and an alternative way of finding such people.

For project management, you'd naturally look for people with a business background or a Master's degree in business. That person may also need to have strong data acumen with experience leading technical projects (even if they are not strictly data-related). Ideally, this would also be someone who has a solid understanding of data strategy.

For someone to manifest the data analysis or BI skillset, you'd look for individuals with a combination of math and business backgrounds. Ideally, someone who also knows how to code, even if it's some high-level language, such as Python or Julia. As long as that person can work the spreadsheets, query a database, present insights, and collaborate effectively with other data professionals.

People embodying the data science skillset aren't that different. The key difference is that such individuals have a stronger STEM background and are better at programming (sometimes in low-level languages software developers use). Data scientists are not engineers, but they may often undertake data engineering tasks if no one else is there for that job. Also, contrary to what many people think, data scientists are business savvy and can interface with non-technical professionals. So, look for such people for this kind of role.

Professionals good at data engineering are similar to data scientists but with a much stronger emphasis on programming. They usually come from an engineering background and often have computer science degrees. Their work is "closer to the metal," and they better understand the tech used in a data project than anyone else.

AI expertise requires those on the cutting edge of this technology. They may not be as savvy in data models as data science professionals, but they tend to understand the field well. They can come from various STEM backgrounds and may have doubled in research. However, the AI professionals who deliver the most value in a data project are not academics. Instead, they are grounded individuals who understand what counts as a useful model or process and are not afraid to get their hands dirty. Beware of people who market themselves as AI experts when all they can do is use ChatGPT well. These are more like prompt engineers, and although they are useful to have around, they are not the same as AI experts (more on that in Chapter 13).

People who encapsulate data visualization in their work tend to be a crossover between data professionals and artists. They are good with numbers and some coding (e.g., JavaScript, as most data visualization programming libraries are in that language) but also great at engaging with their audience. They are an interesting mix of a maven and a salesperson (based on Malcolm Gladwell's taxonomy). Such individuals may have any kind of background and a certain kind of charisma that enables them to make their results accessible and marketable.

3.4 Can you train or educate your existing team members?

If you are dismayed about the talent market or find that the recruiting process is too time-consuming and often not worth the effort, there is another way to get a particular skillset under your team's belt. You can train or educate your existing team members or other professionals in your organization that can be assigned to a data team.

Training talent isn't always easy and in many cases, it's inefficient. Although everyone seems trainable and eager to learn new things when starting a job, they may not always keep up this mentality. This is natural as employees specialize and optimize specific processes to ensure they deliver their regular tasks efficiently. However, a few individuals have some kind of ambition, a drive that regularly prompts them out of their comfort zone. Such people are trainable and easy to educate (a good ROI in the corresponding investment). Some may take educational initiatives themselves by attending (professional) conferences, workshops, seminars, professional Meetup events, and even courses (online or in-person). Although the presence of such individuals in the office may be daunting for some, when leveraged properly, these can be thought leaders who can help drive positive organizational change. Such individuals can foster a different mindset and create a new culture related to data savviness (data literacy). This strategy for training people is more organic and impactful in the long term.

If no such individuals are found, that's still OK. You can be the first such person! If you are not data savvy enough, start by educating yourself. It's much easier than educating others and often as enjoyable. Mind you, you don't need to become an expert before you can pass the torch to others. Ideally, this would happen relatively naturally as others may follow your example. If it doesn't, or you don't want to wait for this to happen, you can actively encourage others to attend particular educational events, call in a professional trainer, or organize a workshop where you share and discuss what you've learned. This can be a great opportunity to practice all the new know-how you attained from this book!

So, to answer the original question of this section, yes, you can definitely train and educate existing team members. Even if not everyone is passionate about data work, everyone can develop some competencies and eventually participate in a data project in some capacity. Are you up for the challenge?

3.5 How does mastery of certain skills come into play?

Mastery is of paramount importance when embodying a certain skillset in data work. Nowadays, everyone can spin a script (not always by typing it themselves), call a few programming libraries, and spit out some numbers. Being able to do all this coherently, responsibly, and easily is a completely different story. The difference between the first data person and the data professional is *mastery*. This doesn't mean that this latter person needs to have some advanced academic qualifications, but a certain mindset. This is something that unfortunately comes with experience or a deep understanding of the subject, and it's not something that you can pick up through a boot camp, an online course, or a book.

In pragmatic terms, mastery translates into efficiencies at work, effective synergy, and flexibility (as well as adaptability). When someone thinks of mastery in martial arts, individuals like Bruce Lee usually come to mind. This martial artist had learned all the main forms available to him and even developed some new ones along with a whole philosophy around the craft. In data work, it's not any different, though it is less film-worthy. After all, the only stuff data professionals crunch are numbers (and data in general) and they do that without vibrant cries accompanying punches and kicks. It's not uncommon for a master data professional to exhibit the kind of creativity that Bruce Lee had or an in-depth understanding of the field (the philosophy mentioned previously). That's not to say that you must have people like that in your data team, but having people aspiring to that ideal is undoubtedly useful. This commitment to excellence that many recruiters seek in candidates stems directly from one's aspirations and this may count more than all the badges in the world that someone may have earned on Kaggle.

In practice, for a data professional to be adept at their skillset, they need to express their role with their work. A data analyst, for example, would provide an insight-rich spreadsheet that's easy to understand and convey the additional work they've done to make it possible. This work would include talking to various people in the organization, gathering all the necessary data, and communicating everything effectively to all the stakeholders. The results would speak for themselves.

To cultivate this mastery mindset, you can look at your data professionals not just as what they are but what they could be if they applied themselves. Inspire and lead them, encouraging their curiosity and self-worth through their discipline. Help them realize that it's not just the data project that matters but also who they become and their own evolution as professionals. The data project is also important, but it is more of an expression of their development and work. Not everything they do will make it to the final product and presentations, but nothing will go to waste. They don't just work for the stakeholders but also for themselves through their development as professionals.

3.6 What is the value of the right skillsets?

This question may be the last one in this chapter, but it could have easily been the first. However, it is the last one for a good reason: it's easy to lose sight of it and get tangled in the plethora of skills, abilities, and the like, that you come across as you build a data team. That's why it's good to remind yourself (and all those partaking in your initiatives) that the right skillsets carry a real value that transcends that of the individual skills involved.

So, what is this value in practice? In a nutshell, it's the mindset of those professionals. No matter what role they play, no matter what their background, they are competent knowledge workers, turning data and information into knowledge and beyond. They are responsible for handling data and know how to avoid the pitfalls accompanying data work. We often hear about data privacy breaches happening, even in large enterprises. These are not always the responsibility of adept hackers, but also a matter of improper application of data security and privacy protocols. Someone with the right skillset in data work can foresee and largely avoid such liabilities.

The value of the right skillsets is also found in the value derived through the data projects at play. If a data project is on time, on budget, and delivers what it set out to deliver, that's a sign that the right skillsets are in place. Even if you don't leverage every skillset described in Figure 3.1, it's fine, as long as you have all the ones you need for the projects. And as your team delivers more and more value, you can grow it, encompassing more skillsets, as needed.

3.7 Key takeaways

- **The phrase "two heads are better than one" applies here**: successful data teams rarely consist of a single person, so it's often beneficial to collaborate with others who bring different skillsets and perspectives.

- **Skillset Profiles**:

    o Project Management:
    - Business background or Master's degree in Project Management.
    - Strong data acumen and experience leading technical projects.
    - Understanding of Data Strategy.
    o Data Analysis/Business Intelligence (BI):
    - Combination of math and business backgrounds.
    - Ability to code (even high-level languages) and work with spreadsheets and databases, delivering insights.
    - Collaboration skills with other data professionals.
    o Data Science:
    - Strong STEM background.
    - Programming skills in low-level languages used by software developers.
    - Business savvy and ability to interface with non-technical professionals.
    o Data Engineering:
    - Engineering background or degree in Computer Science.

- Emphasis on programming and understanding of technology used in data projects.
- "Closer to the metal" than other data professionals.
  - AI Expertise:
    - Traditional tech professional on the cutting edge of AI technology.
    - Good understanding of the AI field, but not in an academic fashion.
    - Ability to deliver value by creating useful models or processes.
  - Data Visualization:
    - Crossover between data professionals and artists.
    - Strong numbers skills and some coding ability (e.g., JavaScript).
    - Charisma and ability to engage with the audience to make results accessible and marketable.

- **Training challenges:**

  - Not everyone is trainable or eager to learn new things.
  - Employees tend to specialize and optimize specific processes, making it difficult to train them.

- **Identifying trainable individuals:**

  - Look for individuals with ambition and drive who are willing to step out of their comfort zone.
  - These individuals can be thought leaders who help drive positive change in the organization.

- **Leading by Example:**

  - o If there are no trainable individuals in the organization, leaders can take the initiative to educate themselves first.
  - o This can be a natural way for others to follow suit, as people learn from examples.

- **Mastery**: Crucial aspect of embodying a skillset in data work. It means having a certain mindset, not just advanced academic qualifications. It's something that comes with experience or deep understanding of the subject.

- **Pragmatic Expression of Mastery**: Data professionals who are masters of their craft can express their role through their work, making it easy for others to understand and appreciate their contributions.

- **The right skillsets' value**: Having the right skillset in data work transcends individual skills and provides a mindset of competence, responsibility, and knowledge workers who can turn data into actionable insights.

- **Measuring success in a data team**: A team's value is measured by delivering projects on time, on budget, and meeting expectations. Having the necessary skills for a project is sufficient, and the team can grow and adapt as needed to deliver more value. The right skillset helps you avoid liabilities.

FOUR

What can you learn about what was or what is right now?

"The master key of knowledge is, indeed, a persistent and frequent questioning."

Peter Abelard

4.1 What picture can data paint for you?

Data can do a lot of things through corresponding projects and one of the lowest-hanging fruits is descriptive analytics. This is a still picture that the data paints for you, giving you an idea of where you were and where you are as an organization. You can think of it as a snapshot of your organization's facets, or perhaps even an MRI scan (depending on how deep the data available is). Such a picture can bring insights about specific conditions, such as particular KPIs, to your awareness. It's a great way to put together useful scorecards that you can use to update stakeholders on how a given feature, product, product line, or even department is doing. If this information is insightful enough, it's likely to help drive action and facilitate decisions.

An example of descriptive analytics in practice is combining various tables related to sales and customer data in a database. This can help you figure out things like "customers who live in location X tend to buy product Y" or "sales in the past year have increased x%" or even things like "product Z is popular mostly people in their 30s." All these insights come about through descriptive analytics.

Descriptive analytics is also a good first step, often necessary, before you embark on other, more ambitious data projects. It doesn't require a lot of resources (in terms of data, people, and computing power), making it ideal for proof-of-concept projects. This is particularly useful when setting up an analytics team or department in your organization.

You can find an overview of descriptive analytics in Figure 4.1.

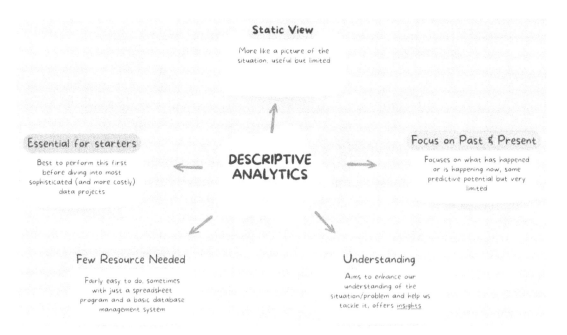

Figure 4.1: Descriptive analytics overview.

4.2 How and when is descriptive analytics useful?

Despite being a low-hanging fruit, descriptive analytics can be immensely useful in relation to other data analytics methodologies. But how and when it can be a value-add is not trivial. Let's look into it in some depth.

First and foremost, descriptive analytics provides us with context. Namely, it helps the organization understand its overall state of being through the various insights it provides related to past performance, KPIs, etc. This also enables better decision making, even if it's only one factor in this process.

Identifying trends and patterns is another aspect of descriptive analytics' usefulness. Through the analysis of historical data, an organization can identify trends and patterns in the market, key metrics, etc. Such insights can inform future actions and strategies when combined with other relevant information.

Descriptive analytics also informs goal-setting in an organization. Providing a baseline for setting goals and objectives (especially in data-driven processes) ensures that targets are realistic and achievable, facilitating leadership and management.

Enhancing communication is another vertical of descriptive analytics' usefulness. By creating scorecards and dashboards, this analytics methodology fosters effective communication regarding key performance metrics.

Root Cause Analysis (RCA) is one of the most challenging kinds of analysis. Fortunately, descriptive analytics can make RCA more accessible. Analyzing relevant descriptive data allows an organization to identify the root causes of issues and take corrective action to improve outcomes.

Prioritizing is an essential part of management, but it can be challenging when many items are involved. Descriptive analytics can facilitate this process and provide a clearer understanding of an organization's SWOT analysis. This can enable informed prioritization of resources and initiatives in the organization.

Finally, another aspect of descriptive analytics' usefulness is fostering a data culture in an organization. This relatively simple methodology is also more accessible to various knowledge workers and management, making the barrier to entry in the world of data a lower one. Thus, it enables data-driven decision making, prioritization, and informed action while eliminating any prejudices related to data work.

As for when descriptive analytics is applicable, this is fairly simple: always. As long as you have some data (it doesn't have to be a lot, nowhere near what counts as Big Data), you can apply this analytics methodology and gain some value from the data at hand. To facilitate all this, it's important to create an infrastructure for this kind of data work and drive relevant initiatives around it. Let's delve more into it now.

4.3 What specific methods and processes can you leverage?

Descriptive analytics is a methodology that encompasses various methods and processes that enable you to process the data effectively and efficiently.

Descriptive analytics includes descriptive stats. Many people are familiar with mean (average) and standard deviation (a measure of dispersion), but there are many more. Each one of these statistics provides a different perspective on the variables analyzed. They can help us identify outliers, for example, which are of particular interest to many people. Wouldn't you want to know if a handful of clients make way more orders than everyone else? And if a particular computer accesses your website far too often, wouldn't you want to know that and perhaps take action (e.g., find out who the person behind that machine is and what they are looking for)? Descriptive stats enable you to find answers to questions like these and more.

Descriptive analytics also entails A-B tests and a series of other statistical tests that enable you to make comparisons objectively. A-B tests, in particular, are very popular in comparing all kinds of continuous variables (e.g., the time someone spends on your landing page, the revenue from sales in a particular branch, etc.). This can make decisions related to some very tricky topics much easier. Even decisions related to website design, for example, can be tackled with this method, helping you figure out if color X is more attractive than color Y for your particular users, when it comes to getting those visitors to order something or turn themselves into leads. Other statistical tests may also add value, in their own way, by shedding some light on things like "How big a factor is X in a particular model?"

Another way to compare continuous variables with each other is through correlation analysis, which is one of the most popular methods in descriptive analytics. Although the adage says that correlation doesn't equal causation, it's still very useful to know if X is correlated to Y. After all, even if correlation doesn't mean causation, it may still imply it. You'll need to run a more in-depth analysis to ensure that X is a root cause of Y, but correlation analysis can be a good starting point. Besides, it's challenging to build any meaningful models based on your data without understanding how correlated the variables of this data are.

Data visualization is also part of descriptive analytics, even if these days it's a field of its own. This is very useful for creating eye-catching graphics to share with stakeholders and as part of an analyst's exploration of the data, aka Exploratory Data Analysis (EDA). Even basic plots that show data distribution are enough to give someone an idea about the variable(s) as a whole and drive that person's next steps. Data visualization is also very useful for developing graphics to include in reports, making the whole reporting process much easier for the analysts.

Descriptive analytics also includes more complex processes, like data mining and cluster analysis. Data mining is the process of finding patterns in data, usually in an automated way. It's also under the EDA umbrella and is often seen as the precursor of data science. Even if it doesn't get as much attention nowadays, its methods are still useful and can add value in various ways, particularly in complex datasets. For instance, if certain customers order product X alongside products Y and Z, this can be expressed as an association rule. The latter is one of the data mining results and is created automatically. Of course, this is not a steadfast rule, but it's more of an observation that gives us insight into customer behavior. This way, if product X doesn't sell particularly well, you can offer it as part of a bundle with Y and Z at a discounted price. This way, you won't have to worry about the stock of X cluttering your warehouse for long.

As for cluster analysis, or clustering, this involves finding groups in a given dataset, usually using the distances among the data points as a similarity metric. In other words, it's the algorithmic way of applying the old adage, "Birds of a feather flock together," and figuring out what these groupings are as well as other relevant information around them. Wouldn't you be curious to know the main customer groups in your organization? Or what are the key groupings of respondents in a survey you've conducted? For questions like that, clustering has the answers. In the hands of a knowledgeable analyst, particularly a data scientist, this can be a very powerful process that can take analytics to a whole new level.

4.4 What are the methods and processes limitations?

As with everything else, there are a number of limitations to the methods and processes of descriptive analytics. This concerns everyone involved in a data project, not just the data professionals.

First and foremost, descriptive analytics tends to focus on the past most and, to some extent, the present. This makes all the methods and processes involved somewhat limited in their scope. In other words, they may not be able to yield any meaningful prediction. For that, there is another methodology called Predictive Analytics, which will be covered in detail in the next chapter.

What's more, just like the vast majority of statistical methods and processes, those of descriptive analytics can be misled by biases in the data. This is something prevalent in analytics in general, though in advanced analytics, it's possible to pinpoint and, to some extent, eliminate those biases. In any case, biases tend to be more of a problem in the fairly simplistic methods descriptive analytics entails, especially the stats-based ones.

Additionally, although it's not an enormous issue, the data involved often requires some pre-processing work (e.g., data wrangling, data cleaning, etc.) before using it in the various methods and processes. This is inevitable in other analytics methodologies, too, and often constitutes most of the time spent on a data project (around 80%). So, if your analysts don't yield any insights immediately, it is probably because they are still cleaning and organizing the data they have to work with.

Moreover, although there is no doubt about the usefulness of descriptive analytics, this methodology may not always yield something particularly interesting or actionable. This could be due to various factors, the most likely one being that the signal isn't there in the data. However, such a limitation shouldn't dissuade you or the data workers involved as it's not uncommon and usually not anyone's fault. In cases like this, an experienced data professional from outside the organization can help shed some light on the issue and develop potential solutions.

Furthermore, due to its simplicity, descriptive analytics may seem too trivial to justify having a whole team in this area. This is particularly the case when the organization doesn't have a data culture yet or there isn't enough budget for data initiatives. This doesn't mean anything, however, since sometimes the biggest value-adds are in more advanced analytics that rely on the descriptive analytics work that paves the way.

4.5 What are some potential pitfalls in this methodology?

Beyond the limitations mentioned in the previous section, which are usually unavoidable, there are also some potential pitfalls regarding descriptive analytics.

However, these are often within your locus of control, so raising awareness about them can help you and your team tackle or even prevent them altogether.

For instance, there are data quality issues. Descriptive analytics will produce misleading results if the data is incomplete, inaccurate, or inconsistent. You can tackle this pitfall by ensuring high-quality data and closely examining biases in the data.

Lack of contextual understanding is another issue that may arise from descriptive analytics. Without sufficient context, this methodology might not provide meaningful insights, or the insights may be hard-pressed to drive action. Understanding the organization's goals, objectives, and key performance indicators is essential as such awareness helps bring to mind the bigger picture, which may be elusive to the data professionals involved.

Another pitfall of descriptive analytics is insufficient interpretation. The outputs of this methodology can be complex and need interpretation to be made relevant. Organizations must have the necessary skills and resources to effectively analyze and apply these findings, which the data analysts may not always be equipped to do. Proper communication among all the stakeholders can help alleviate this issue.

Complacency is an additional pitfall of descriptive analytics and analytics in general. Relying too heavily on this methodology might lead to complacency. This may express itself as a more reactive approach to whatever happens. Using these insights as a starting point for further exploration and action is essential, rather than becoming stuck in the status quo.

Finally, overemphasis on historical data is yet another pitfall of the methodology that is also challenging to overcome. Descriptive analytics focuses on past performance, but this might not translate to future success. In a world riddled with unforeseeable events, it's hard to prepare if all we have is data reflecting the past (such events are often referred to as *Black Swans*, a term coined by N. Taleb). Organizations must balance historical insights with forward-looking perspectives, such as predictive and prescriptive analytics. This may not help us prevent Black Swans, but we can at least have some heads-up that can enable us to mitigate the negative effects of such events.

4.6 Who can you leverage for this kind of work?

To be pragmatic about this data initiative, we also need to look at it from a human resources perspective. So, before you ask your HR rep to put together an ad for such a professional, it's good to see what such professionals may be already in your organization. Depending on your budget, you may want to supplement that workforce with additional assets, ideally people well-versed in analytics, ideally from a technical background (instead of just people who have done some bootcamp online and have no idea how to apply analytics in practice).

Specifically, you may want to look into data analysts. These are people who are either versed in the data analysis skillset mentioned in the previous chapter, or junior level data scientists looking to gather some experience in the field. If you opt for the latter, you may run a slightly higher risk as they may not linger in this role for very long, but they may be a great investment should you wish to have a more diverse and more advanced data team one day. Opt for people who have at least a degree (ideally from a STEM discipline), have attended an immersive course in analytics, have invested in books/videos from a reliable publisher, and have some experience with data projects (even if the latter are based on coursework from the course they'd attended).

Business intelligence professionals are also a good option for someone who wants to delve into descriptive analytics. As a bonus, such people are better-versed in business processes, tend to have some domain knowledge, and may be familiar with analytics from a very practical perspective. If these professionals can supplement their skillset with some programming, they may be able to undertake the data analyst role and gain some good insights.

Other data professionals are also an option. Even if they are not geared towards analytics, specifically, if they have worked with data they probably already have most of the skills required. If you have such professionals in your workforce and they have the bandwidth, you can also leverage them in descriptive analytics. Some training first is bound to go a long way, however.

Finally, anyone knowledgeable in analytics to some extent, especially if they are willing to learn, is another option. This is particularly the case if you have underutilized employees or generalists who have an interest in data work. You can work with them and help them develop their expertise as long as they are trainable.

4.7 Key takeaways

- **Descriptive analytics** is a fundamental data methodology that provides *insights* into where an organization has been and where it currently stands, using data to paint a picture (or take a snapshot).

- **Value of descriptive analytics**: A good first step before embarking on more complex data projects, requiring minimal resources (data, people, computing power). Ideal for proof-of-concept projects or setting up an analytics team/department within an organization.

- **Descriptive analytics is useful in the following ways**:

  o   Providing context.
  o   Identifying trends and patterns.
  o   Informing goal setting.
  o   Enhancing communication.
  o   Supporting root cause analysis.

- Facilitating prioritization.
- Creating a foundation of understanding of the status quo.

- **Methods and processes in descriptive analytics:**

  - Descriptive stats.
  - A-B testing and other statistical tests.
  - Correlation analysis.
  - Data visualization.
  - Data mining.
  - Cluster analysis.

- **Key limitations of descriptive analytics:**

  - Focus on the past and the present mostly.
  - Can be misled by biases.
  - Require some pre-processing work beforehand (e.g., data wrangling).
  - May not yield something especially interesting or actionable always.
  - May seem too trivial to justify having a whole team in this area.

- **Potential pitfalls of descriptive analytics:**

  - Data quality issues.
  - Lack of contextual understanding.
  - Insufficient interpretation.
  - Complacency.
  - Overemphasis on historical data.

- **People you can leverage in descriptive analytics:**

  - o Data analysts.
  - o BI professionals.
  - o Other data professionals (e.g., entry-level data scientists).
  - o Anyone knowledgeable in analytics to some extent.

FIVE

What can you learn about what is bound to be?

"The one who knows all the answers has not been asked all the questions."

Confucius

5.1 Is it possible to predict the future using data?

This may sound philosophical, but the whole prediction business has been at the forefront of science since the days of Aristarchus.[5] It's not a coincidence that this line of scientific research brought about a series of mathematical laws when Kepler finished his great work on the subject, enabling scientists to predict the location of various celestial bodies in our solar system. This is all fairly well-known historical information. What's not so well-known is that Kepler relied heavily on data from Tycho Brahe, a Danish astronomer who meticulously

---

[5] One of the greatest astronomers and mathematicians of antiquity. Born in Samos around 310 BCE, he was one of the first scientists to propose the heliocentric model of the solar system (centuries before Copernicus and Kepler). You may have heard of him from the film *Agora* where he is shown working together with Hypatia, although there is no historical evidence of him ever living there for long. His model of the celestial bodies enabled astronomers to make fairly accurate predictions about eclipses, which was a remarkable feat at the time.

collected a lot of data based on the observations conducted by the astronomical observatory where he worked. This may not seem like a big deal in the context of today's datascape, but considering how you'd have to make all your calculations by hand back then, it wasn't easy. This example shows that making predictions based on data has been possible for centuries using data and math (even without computers!). This clearly shows that working the data to predict the future is a matter of mindset and mental discipline. Naturally, you'd expect this trend to continue and grow in power and scope now that we have sophisticated machines to do all the calculations, allowing us to focus more on this methodology's conceptual and design elements.

Back to our reality, making predictions using data has been a powerful methodology in data work and is often called *predictive analytics*. As a methodology, it's more advanced and enables us to foresee the future (in some aspects) and prepare for it. Because of the complexity of the models involved, it tends to be heavier on the required resources (meaning that it can get expensive if you want the predictions to be more accurate or more long-term). However, it gives us a more dynamic view of whatever it analyzes, making the insights that derive from it more impactful. You can view the key aspects of the predictive analytics methodology in Figure 5.1.

In this chapter, we'll explore this methodology, answering questions about its usefulness, what methods or processes it entails, its limitations, the risks of the methodology, and the people you would need to conduct this kind of data work.

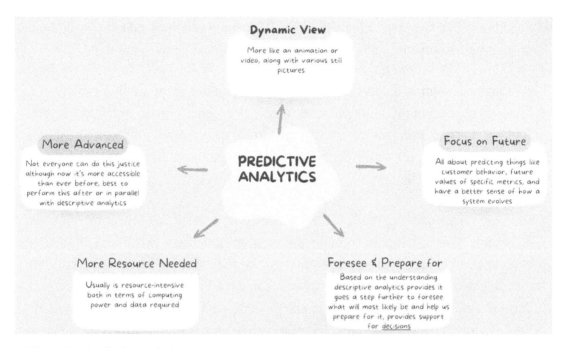

Figure 5.1: Predictive analytics overview.

5.2 How and when is predictive analytics useful?

Just like with descriptive analytics, predictive analytics can be useful in particular use cases that lend themselves to this kind of data analysis. Beyond these use cases, there are also specific value-adds that this methodology entails that put the corresponding data to good use. Whenever, for example, there is a need for forecasting, particularly in scenarios involving complex relationships among variables, predictive analytics can be a great value-add to your organization. Forecasting always has a temporal element to it, making it a very applicable method, especially when time-stamped data comes into play.

Enhanced customer insights are another situation where predictive analytics shines. This goes beyond the basic segmentation of your customer base into categories that derive from a number of filters in a spreadsheet. Customer insights derive from an intelligent grouping of customers based on a number of dynamic and a few static characteristics. This often involves making predictions of their future behavior and getting a better idea of what makes them tick.

Risk management is also very relevant when it comes to predictive analytics. It involves quantifying risk, in whatever way it is expressed in an organization, and finding ways to mitigate or at least handle it effectively. This whole process involves a lot of data and predictive models. After all, risk refers to future situations, so what better way to apply this future-predicting methodology?

In every organization, various operations often need optimization. This is something you can model through the data around these processes. Predictive analytics can enable business operations to be managed by better understanding the patterns they entail. This way, you can avoid running out of stock for a particular product, for example, and ensure there aren't too many inefficiencies in your supply chains. Naturally, similar value-adds can be found in internal processes, such as handling cash flows efficiently, optimizing marketing campaigns, etc.

Predictive analytics can also offer a competitive advantage, particularly when competitors don't use this methodology. It may seem strange, but many organizations are still data illiterate, and their use of analytics is rudimentary, if used at all. Although this is still better than nothing, it's hard to imagine how an organization like that can compete with an organization that employs predictive analytics in various projects.

One of the key areas where predictive analytics can be a value-add is that of cost savings. Although this is covered in part through the other value-adds mentioned here, it's important to highlight that there are tangible benefits to the bottom line whenever predictive analytics is applied properly. Predictive analytics can help eliminate inefficiencies, improve marketing, and design better products or services.

A lot has been said and written about decision making and there is even a field in this area (Decision Science). Yet, despite all the new terms used these days, it's still an established procedure. Even if traditional decision making links to intangible things like intuition, psychology, and reading between the lines, it would be naive to rely on those primarily. Predictive analytics is essential for making better decisions, particularly for complex scenarios involving ample data points. Complementary to decision science techniques, as well as the human factor, it can improve the whole process and, most importantly, provide a more objective framework to leverage with all stakeholders.

Beyond these value-adds of predictive analytics, there are more that may not be as important or fairly easy to deduce based on what we've discussed. Predictive analytics can benefit enhanced compliance (particularly when dealing with sensitive data or data related to PII[6]), innovative product development, and Return on Investment (ROI) analysis.

But when would you want to apply predictive analytics, in practice, to provide these value-adds? Usually, you'd do that for specific use cases, such as:

- Sales forecasting
- Customer (or employee) churn prediction
- Fraud detection and prevention
- Credit risk assessment
- Inventory management and optimization

---

[6] Personally Identifiable Information. This involves variables that can give away someone's identity, especially when they are combined together through the use of some advanced predictive model. PII leakage is a serious violation of trust with customers and may even incur fines. The gathering and management of PII-related data needs to be in compliance to specific legislation, such as GDPR and HIPAA, depending on the people and processes involved.

- Supply chain optimization
- Marketing campaign optimization
- Product recommendation engines

Some of these may not apply to your industry, but this list gives you an idea of the use cases that lend themselves to this methodology. Based on this, you can perhaps extrapolate and find use cases more applicable to your work.

5.3 What specific methods and processes can you leverage?

That's a question that may concern mostly data professionals who work in predictive analytics. However, to better understand such professionals and enable better communication, it is best to be familiar with the methods and processes this methodology entails. You don't need to understand all the technical intricacies, but getting an idea of what they do and when they are relevant can help optimize their usage in data projects and foster synergy between management and data workers.

The most commonly used method in predictive analytics is classification/regression. Some people distinguish between the two, but in essence, they both use data models (mostly machine learning, AI-based, and Stats) to predict a given variable. Classification is used if this variable is discreet (e.g., whether a customer will buy product A, product B, or nothing at all). If the variable is continuous (e.g., How much money is a given customer going to spend during their website visit?), regression comes into play. Naturally, the two methods are not the same technically, but it's often the case that if someone can work well with the data at hand, they can leverage both equally well.

Clustering is another method in predictive analytics, though it is used somewhat differently here. It is often part of a larger data model or even as a pre-processing step. For example, you may leverage clustering for better feature engineering, which is essential when you have a lot of data points in your data project.

Additionally, clustering can be used effectively for anomaly detection. The latter is particularly useful in cases where you wish to isolate instances of bizarre or problematic behavior in your organization, be it someone visiting your website far more than usual, excessive charges from a vendor, etc. Since anomalies are fairly rare, it's extremely difficult to model them using classification, which is why alternative approaches, like clustering, are used instead.

Time Series Analysis (TSA) is another method under the predictive analytics umbrella. As the name suggests, it involves analyzing the various elements in a time series and making predictions. This may seem straightforward when learning about it in a textbook, but these time series are quite complex in practice, and the relationships involved aren't easy to model. Contrary to what some analysts believe, stats-based methods are not the best way to go in such scenarios, although they are a good starting point. Nowadays, ML- and AI-based models are the most popular.

Recommendation systems are a popular process involved in predictive analytics, particularly in content-related websites and e-commerce ones. You may have used such a system when browsing for books on Amazon or at your favorite article platform (e.g., Medium). These systems take into account your preferences (if they have a record of them), your activity (e.g., the last item you browsed), and what other people did when they were in a similar situation (particularly people who have a similar user profile), and make a number of suggestions accordingly. It's similar to a classification system, though it uses various data points while leveraging different kinds of user behavior.

Natural Language Processing (NLP) is another method in predictive analytics that involves working with text data. So, if you have web forms or open-ended questions in a survey, that's what you would use to make sense of them without having to read them one by one. These days, NLP is largely outsourced to Large Language Models (LLMs). Yet, if you don't have access to an LLM or have privacy concerns with the ones you find online, it's good to be aware of the NLP alternative, which is something you have full control over, along with a sense of transparency. NLP can also work in conjunction with LLMs to process their outputs.

Survival analysis, which involves modeling the time it takes for an event to occur (or not to occur), is another method under the predictive analytics umbrella. Although we use it most in the finance industry, it's still useful to know as it may have applications elsewhere, even in places you wouldn't expect.[7]

5.4 What are the methods and processes limitations?

Despite their benefits, the methods and processes in predictive analytics are not without their shortcomings. The most notable is the black-box nature of most algorithms. This is particularly the case with algorithms based on artificial neural networks. The worst part is that due to the nature of such systems, it's really hard to overcome this issue unless using an altogether novel design or architecture. The black-box algorithms make it very challenging to:

- Understand the connection between inputs and outputs
- Explain how they arrive at the conclusions they arrive
- Debug them if they yield inaccurate results
- Pinpoint the presence of biases in the whole process and deal with them

Data quality issues are another concern in predictive analytics, though they aren't directly related to the methods or processes mentioned previously. Data quality involves the data itself and encompasses all kinds of methodologies used.

---

[7] During his time at Georgia Tech, the author was closely involved in a project for the DoD involving survival analysis.

Predictive analytics models tend to be fairly loose with their assumptions as they don't understand context the way we do. As a result, they may have unreliable assumptions in their workflow, which will often appear in their outputs. Combined with their limitations regarding domain knowledge, this whole matter is best handled by people familiar with the bigger picture, not just the nuts and bolts of the predictive analytics models at play.

The computational intensity of the predictive analytics methods is also a limitation. It's not that the intensity is such that you will not be able to use those methods; after all, there is always the cloud where most of the computational heavy lifting happens. However, this intensity translates into costs that can accumulate quickly and, at the very least, may drive down the ROI of the data projects entailing predictive analytics.

Despite all their great benefits, predictive analytics models have a somewhat limited ability to generalize beyond the data they are trained on. Even if the data is of good quality, they may still drop in their performance over time as the data at hand becomes less and less relevant for the predictions made (called *data drift*). Additionally, the environment (e.g., market) may change over time, making users change their behavior (e.g., through the presence of new options). This phenomenon, aka concept drift, is beyond the data, although it definitely affects it. As a result, you have to develop several models, sometimes based on the same kind of data points, just to keep those predictions relevant (model maintenance and updates), which is a good remedy to data and concept drifts.

Unfairness and (often hidden) biases are another limitation of predictive analytics systems. It's not that they set out to be unfair or biased, but sometimes they just don't know any better. More often than not, this is due to biases in the data that's used to train them, or the data professional's inability to use some heuristics to detect, gauge, and manage said biases. Nevertheless, the limitation still affects the methodology as a whole since pre-processing the data is an inherent part of it, too.

Finally, another limitation is the lack of human judgment in the methods and processes of predictive analytics. This is not the fault of the methodology itself, however. Plus, it's unlikely that it will evolve to tackle this issue. More often than not, it's a management problem for getting the wrong people involved in the whole process. The good news is that it's easily fixable once you identify it and get people with better judgment involved in your organization's predictive analytics projects.

5.5 What risks are there in predictive analytics?

Hopefully, the limitations of the methods and processes of this methodology mentioned in the previous section will help you better understand the field. But how do these translate into specific risks in the organization? Let's find out.

First of all, predictive analytics tends to be quite confident about its predictions, fostering a kind of overconfidence about the future in all the people involved. This includes both the data workers and the managers of the corresponding projects. Coupled with the fairly limited understanding of how probabilities work and how they are often misused to express some subjective measure of confidence in predictions, this whole matter can easily get out of hand. Even if a predictive model is 100% certain about a certain event in the future, it's good to remember that this is still a guess, not some prophesy.

The lack of transparency we alluded to in the previous section is also a serious risk of this methodology. Although this doesn't apply to every single method or process involved (e.g., decision tree classifiers and regressors are as transparent as can be), most of the modern models used tend to have this issue. The worst part is that this lack of transparency will not go away any time soon since even if there are transparent alternatives, chances are that the edge in accuracy that non-transparent models offer makes them preferable.

A relatively hidden risk of predictive analytics is the risk of a lower ROI in some cases. It could be that the data at hand doesn't have a strong enough signal to make reliable predictions for your organization's particular use cases. The models themselves may be fine (i.e., they were developed with good practices in mind), but if the data is information-poor (like some watered-down gasoline), the data project's ROI will suffer.

Finally, there is also the risk of excessively relying on predictive analytics models. That's not an issue innate to the methodology but has to do with how the models are marketed to the stakeholders and the whole hype around the field of analytics. The bottom line is that relying on them is fine for situations where you don't have any better options, but relying on them exclusively, especially in an automated way, is a disaster waiting to happen. Fortunately, this can be averted through a more conscious use of this technology and keeping humans in the loop.

5.6 Who can you leverage for this kind of work?

Like in the descriptive analytics methodology, here you have some options, too. Your best bet, however, would be to involve data scientists. Be aware of people who market themselves as data scientists, though, just because they have taken a course at some university, have done a couple of Kaggle projects, or have just completed an online bootcamp. If you have to take a lot of time explaining to someone in this role the business needs and how data work needs to align itself with them, you are probably talking to an imposter.

Apart from data scientists, you can also leverage senior data analysts for this kind of work. Even if their coding skills aren't always on par with those of a data scientist, they are likely to understand enough to be able to add value. Also, they are likely already on a career path toward data science, so they are bound to be a good fit for the role.

Machine Learning (ML) engineers are a relatively new kind of data professionals who are a good match for predictive analytics work. Although they specialize in ML, they tend to have a software engineering background, so they should be able to work well in this role and perhaps even undertake a data engineering role.

Don't let the fact that they may not be as knowledgeable in statistics be a concern. Chances are that you won't be using stats all that much anyway in this methodology.

You can also leverage other data professionals in predictive analytics. As long as they clearly understand what the work entails and are willing to learn what they don't know, they should be productive members of your data team. It would be best if they are involved mostly in supportive roles; however, they should be under the guidance and mentoring of a more knowledgeable data professional who is well-versed in this methodology.

5.7 Key takeaways

- **Predictive analytics** is a powerful methodology in data work that enables us to foresee the future and prepare for it. It also provides a dynamic view of analyzed data, leading to more impactful insights.

- **The usefulness of predictive analytics** involves the following verticals:

    o Improved forecasting.
    o Enhanced customer insights.
    o Risk management.
    o Operational optimization.
    o Competitive advantage.
    o Cost savings.
    o Improved decision making.
    o Enhanced compliance.
    o Innovative product development.
    o Return on Investment (ROI) analysis.

- **Common use cases of predictive analytics today include:**

  - Sales forecasting.
  - Customer churn prediction.
  - Fraud detection and prevention.
  - Credit risk assessment.
  - Inventory management and optimization.
  - Supply chain optimization.
  - Marketing campaign optimization.
  - Product recommendation engines.

- **Methods and processes** of predictive analytics include:

  - Classification/Regression. These include mostly ML models, AI-based models, and a few stats models.
  - Clustering. This is usually part of a larger model or as a pre-processing step, such as feature engineering. Also for anomaly detection.
  - Time Series Analysis (TSA)
  - Recommendation systems.
  - Natural Language Processing (NLP).
  - Survival analysis. This involves modeling the time it takes for an event to occur or not to occur. Common in the finance industry.

- **Typical limitations of predictive analytics methods and processes:**

  - Black box nature of most predictive analytics algorithms.
  - Data quality issues.
  - Risk of model over-fitting due to complexity.
  - Unreliable assumptions.
  - Computational intensity.
  - Domain knowledge limitations.

- o Limited ability to generalize.
- o Biases (usually hidden) and unfairness.
- o Lack of human judgment.
- o Data drift and concept drift.
- o Model maintenance and updates.

- **High-level risks of predictive analytics** include the following:

  - o Overconfidence about the future.
  - o Biases incorporated into decision making.
  - o Lack of transparency.
  - o Risk of a lower ROI in some cases.
  - o Easy to get into excessive reliance on such models.

- **People you can involve in predictive analytics projects and initiatives:**

  - o Data scientists.
  - o Senior data analysts.
  - o ML engineers.
  - o Other data professionals.

PART II

What about the bigger picture?

"There are no foolish questions and no man becomes a fool until he has stopped asking questions."

Charles Proteus Steinmetz

Six

What will you need from data in the foreseeable future?

"The most valuable questions in life are often the ones we never think to ask."

Unknown

6.1 Are you asking the right questions about your projects?

That's a good question and you are probably the best person to answer it. It's not so much the answer itself that matters, but the sense of wandering that comes along with it and the search for the answer itself. In Appendix B, there is a proposed process for tackling any kind of question that is answerable. However, let's look into some relevant matters to facilitate your quest for an answer.

First of all, the world is always changing, and so is the data. Things are not static, even if we often comfort ourselves with the relative stability of our society. Of course, we always compare it with societies in distress or undergoing rapid changes, usually due to geopolitical events. So, even if these matters don't affect our organization directly, they may change the overall global environment (which also seems to change on its own in matters beyond our control). All this brings about shifts in people's behavior along with the data describing it. Since every organization relies on people, these shifts trickle down to the organization itself, the data it ingests, and its processes.

Our data also symbolizes how much we know or the knowledge we have access to. As such, it's limited, but as data is abundant these days, this limit is very soft. It's good to remember that data works well with data it's somewhat related to. Two datasets may look like two different things, but they can be combined if there is even one variable connecting them (usually something like time, order number, etc.). If the analysts involved know what they are doing and why, chances are that you will all see first-hand something beautiful: the synergy of different data points. In practice, this means that you usually get better information and better accuracy in the predictions involved as a direct result of enlarging your original dataset.

Returning to the questions, it's good to remember that some answers (and the actionable information they conceal) may never be revealed unless you ask the right questions about the data involved. And sometimes, the data at hand just isn't enough or isn't the right data for the projects you need, through no fault of anyone in the organization. That's why it's important not just to ask questions but to ask the right questions about the data and to go beyond what's there, imagining what could and should be there, readily available to your dedicated data workers.

In this chapter, we'll look into the kinds of questions you need to be asking about data in general (beyond the data you have already), a few things about automation, the value of building a data culture in your organization, the different levels of data literacy, and whether you can be data-driven in your decisions. Hopefully, you'll be able to find an answer to the original question posed in this section.

6.2 What are the questions to ask beyond the data at hand?

Let's start our investigation by looking at the questions you need to ask about data, not limiting yourself to the data you have access to already.

One fairly obvious question you might ask is, "What else do we need in terms of data?" In other words, is the data at hand enough? Chances are that it's not, while how to supplement it may not be so apparent. More often than not, it's not just more records you need in the corresponding database tables, but also more columns (variables).

"What about data quality?" If quality was a concern before when evaluating the data at hand, it should be more of a concern regarding data outside the organization. In your domain, you may have fail-safes and procedures to ensure a certain standard about the data. Outside it, it's anyone's guess. So, when dealing with data from the outside, especially from places you don't know well, it doesn't hurt to err on the side of caution. After all, low-quality data may not only fail to add any value but may even dilute the quality of your current data.

"What models will we use?". If the data at hand is best utilized with advanced models, like deep learning networks, you may want to stick with that (although it's not a bad idea to try other models, too, with the new data). If that's the case, you may need a large dataset (in terms of records) to supplement the existing data. So, the models you plan to use will be an important factor for the data you may want to acquire. Naturally, this would also be a factor for the professionals and technologies you'll utilize. We'll talk more about this in Chapter 8.

Naturally, at one point, you may want to ask what else there is in terms of data. Things like data governance will then come into consideration. Will you be using the same data architectures in your databases? Or will you need to redesign the architecture or perhaps even create new databases? Where will the data live exactly? How often will it be augmented? These are all considerations that go beyond the basics we have just explored.

Of course, all the additional data in the world wouldn't be as useful if you couldn't integrate it with your existing data. That's also something you may want to ask and investigate. Ideally, you'd look into this matter before getting any new data. Having silos in your data repositories isn't good, especially if you need to pay for this data. Involving a data engineer in this conversation would be useful as they could figure out ways to make this integration possible and even efficient.

Data is great and additional data may make your data team happy. But to ensure that the other stakeholders are happy, too, you'd want to consider the expected benefits of this data (ideally, before you get it). Even if integration is efficient and everyone involved in the ingestion and processing of the data is content, a data project is a success only if it adds value. So, it's good to clarify the value before you transfer a single byte of it through your data pipelines. Will this value translate into financial benefits, better lead generation, and improved efficiencies? How will you measure the return on all this investment?

You may also want to inquire about privacy and data security matters. Not because they are a value-add in themselves but because they are essential. If you neglect them, all the benefits from the data projects made possible with any expansions in your data pipelines will wither away. The more data you have, the better the chances of some of it getting corrupt or, even worse, leaked. That's why it can easily become a liability unless data is governed properly.

Finally, you would also want to ask about the topic of project ownership. It's not enough that someone capable works for a particular project, even if that person coordinates everyone else involved. Someone needs to take ownership and have authority in that team. The idealistic solutions of certain big tech companies where someone "leads through influence only" don't apply in data work. A far more effective way is for one person to be responsible for the project. That person may also be responsible for the project's data along with its security.

In Fig 6.1. you can see an overview of the questions you could ask in relation to data in the future. You can ponder on them and come up with follow-up questions, too.

Figure 6.1: Potential (good) questions about data in the projects to come.

6.3 What about automation?

Everyone has wished at one time or another that a certain menial task be completed magically. Since most people have outgrown the belief in genies, they rely on the magic of technology. Enter the process of automation, which has been touted as one of the many hands-on applications of AI. As such, it is closely related to data. If that's the case, why has it not been included in the book, especially in this chapter?

Automation can leverage software bots, AI agents, and ML systems to handle mundane and/or repetitive tasks. It's not always a data-driven technology, so it's not mentioned previously. However, if it's something you wish to incorporate into your organization, it's good to know more about its value-adds and areas of application, as well as some other matters related to it. After all, it's a broad term, and it's been overhyped for the past few years.

First of all, let's look at the value-related aspects of automation. It can add value in various ways, the most important of which are:

- increased efficiency
- improved accuracy
- cost savings
- scalability
- compliance

Regarding its most common areas of application, these are:

- back-office operations
- customer service
- supply chain management
- marketing
- manufacturing

As expected, not every process can or even should be automated. Even if automation drives efficiency, certain aspects of an organization are better left as they are. There is plenty of room for automation in data work, particularly in processes involving moving data around and performing standard operations. However, processes that involve interfacing with people may be better left as they are since not everyone enjoys talking to a chatbot when trying to solve a problem with their bank account, for example.

The human aspect of automation (which is grossly neglected when people talk about how great this technology is) involves training people to handle the changes it incurs. At the very least, everyone involved in a particular operation needs to know what processes are automated and how. If the customer complaints department isn't aware of the new automation in the organization's website that involves a chatbot that isn't fully operational yet, it's good they get a heads-up.

Robotic Process Automation (RPA) is a subset of automation involving mostly rule-based procedures and has a more narrow scope. RPA is not so popular today, and it mostly leverages software rather than AI. The latter is more popular as a technology and easier to use, though it still requires some work to get it to work properly. Also, although RPA is fairly straightforward regarding the costs involved, AI-based automation can be trickier and is bound to involve subscription fees. We talk more about AI-powered automation in Chapter 11.

6.4 What is the value of developing a data culture?

A data culture is the collective behaviors and beliefs of people who value, practice, and encourage the use of data to improve decision making. However, this goes beyond data workers since it's an attribute of the whole organization.

Having a healthy data culture in your organization can bring about worthwhile benefits, such as a better chance of successful data projects. After all, the synergy between data workers and management often relies on many other people who contribute in their own way to these projects. By having a good data culture in the organization, communication and collaboration among all these people become frictionless and more effective.

A strong data culture can also enable more data-driven (objective) decisions. As this is something we'll cover later in this chapter, it suffices to say that it's a good thing that can help you in many ways. Many people talk about the merits of a data-driven organization, where decisions occur objectively based on data rather than feelings and opinions. Not so many people actually put in the effort it takes to develop a data culture. You could be one of those few who do.

Data culture also fosters a better understanding of how data is a resource, potentially turning it into an asset. If you and the other stakeholders don't understand data in some depth, it's very easy to neglect it and pay more attention to other resources. In that sense, understanding data is equivalent to seeing colors when most people around you are color-blind. This understanding comes about on an organizational scale only through data culture.

Fortunately, there are many data-savvy people who would be interested in helping your organization. They can be vendors, partners, or even contractors. A good data culture allows leveraging them through a mutually beneficial collaboration. Note that many of these people may already be in your organization, even if they don't advertise themselves as such.

Increased transparency and accountability are also a consequence of a good data culture. The latter not only entails getting everyone up to speed on what data can do and how it's useful to the organization, but also keeping accurate records of operations. This alone is enough to promote transparency in whatever happens in the organization to the extent that it doesn't jeopardize sensitive information.

A final benefit of a solid data culture is that of better strategic planning. That is, better decision making on a higher level. Ideally, a data culture would begin at the organization's higher echelons, benefiting it as a whole, instead of just providing marginal benefits to a particular department. One of the best ways data culture benefits a whole organization is by steering it in the right direction at the right time, which is difficult to do without data work.

Just like conventional cultures, a data culture is not homogeneous. To better understand it, it's best to explore the various kinds of people you may find in the world of data. Namely, you'll need to view the world from the angle of data literacy and its various levels.

6.5 What are the different levels of data literacy?

That's a question everyone needs to be asking, regardless of their relationship with data. Just like the literacy related to the language(s) we speak, data literacy is vital, regardless of your role in relation to data. In brief, a popular taxonomy of data literacy levels is the following:

1. **Data novice**. This involves someone very new to the data world. Most children are at this level. The key competencies of the data novice are the abilities to:

   o Understand what data is and its importance.
   o Recognize common data types (e.g., numbers, text, images).
   o Identify the need for data-driven decision making.

2. **Data enthusiast**. This person has a decent understanding of data and may be inclined to play around with a spreadsheet application like MS Excel, Gnumeric, or the spreadsheet program of OnlyOffice. Maybe even do some basic programming to crunch some numbers and get something interesting out of them. This person is not an analyst, but they might become one if they pursue this interest in data. Key abilities include:

   o Interpret basic statistical concepts (mean, median, mode).
   o Understand simple data visualization techniques (charts, graphs).
   o Perform basic calculations and analysis (summarizing data, identifying trends).

3. **Knowledge worker**. This is the typical data analyst and data scientist, depending on their know-how, experience in programming,

and diversity of skills. Knowledge workers may not always carry these specific labels but may also work as decision scientists, BI professionals, etc. This category includes anyone who feels comfortable with data work and can derive some value from it. Key abilities include:

- o Analyze and interpret more complex statistical concepts (correlation, regression).
- o Create and customize advanced data visualizations (e.g., heatmaps, scatter plots).
- o Conduct basic data modeling and predictive analytics.

4. **Data expert (or data educator)**. This is where the more experienced data scientists and AI experts are. Certain data architects/modelers would also be here, though their models would be different and involve different processes. Note that individuals at this level don't need to teach, but they can if needed. So, having at least one of them in a data team is especially useful since they can help develop a data culture in the organization. Key abilities include:

- o Develop and apply sophisticated data models (e.g., machine learning, deep learning).
- o Create complex data visualizations and interactive dashboards.
- o Design and implement large-scale data systems and architectures.

5. **Data professional (aka, data master)**. This is where the most dedicated data professionals find themselves. Data leaders of different types, data mentors (especially those who can mentor all previous kinds of data people), researchers of data technologies, etc., are people of this caliber. Having even one such individual in your team can yield benefits that even a dozen normal data workers would be unable to. When leveraged properly, such an individual can be a

force multiplier and a true asset to your organization. Key abilities include:

- o Lead or participate in multidisciplinary teams to drive data-driven decisions.
- o Develop and mentor others on data literacy skills.
- o Contribute to the development of new data-related tools, technologies, and methodologies.

Note that this taxonomy is for educational purposes only. It's intended to be a good tool for understanding where you and your team members stand and what you need to become more data-savvy. You can learn more about this topic through the excellent book on the subject by Peter Aiken and Todd Harbour.[8]

6.6 Can you be data-driven in your decisions?

Unlike most other questions in this book, this one seems simple. After all, it's a yes-no question that you will answer fairly quickly. However, before you venture into an answer, let's look into the topic more closely, starting with what data-driven means. We briefly discussed it, but what does it mean for your organization and you?

Data-driven usually refers to something supported and often motivated by data and the analysis of it for a particular objective. The problem comes first, then the data, and then the decision. The data alone doesn't do much, apart from giving you some time and highlighting your options. The analytics of this data provide you with the strengths and weaknesses of these options. The decision remains with you.

---

[8] Peter Aiken, Todd Harbour, "Data Literacy: Achieving Higher Productivity for Citizens, Knowledge Workers, and Organizations", Technics Publications, 2021.

Data-driven decisions are preferable, but how are they better? Data is more objective as it grows in size and more intelligent models process it. Can you claim to have all the data you need and those models in your head? If not, you are better off getting that data and analyzing it methodically through the analytics methodologies we've viewed in previous chapters. Then, you can have, at the very least, better support for whatever you decide. You may still arrive at the right decision on your own. Having the support of a data-driven process, however, would make this decision more confident and easier to communicate to everyone else involved. If the decision data dictates is different from what you intuited, that's still good, as it can help you explore a different approach and perhaps learn something you wouldn't be able to learn otherwise.

Before you opt for data-driven decision making, here are some questions you need to ask yourself:

- Do we have the data needed to explore the decision space?
- Is analytics sufficient, or should we look into decision science instead?
- Is there a way to combine the two approaches?
- How can we collect relevant data for decisions like this in the future?
- What subject matter experts can we bring into this to gather relevant information?
- How do we store and utilize such information in the future?
- How do we know that the data and information gathered are of high enough veracity?

Keep an open mind and explore the topic with a sense of curiosity. Data is important as a resource, but its role is to serve your decision making, not the other way around!

Theoretically, you can be data-driven, no doubt about that. But what about being that in practice? You are at a good place if you can find good answers to the questions above. This is just the beginning, though. After all, question creation is a skill that needs practice, just like everything else. When the questions you leverage drive good decisions and utilize data intelligently, you'll have the feedback you need to assess the answers and, more importantly, the questions themselves.

Hopefully, by now, you'll have found an answer to your question about whether or not you are asking the right questions. Whatever it is, you don't have to share it with anyone right now. Like any useful information, it is better off being acted upon. What decisions can you make based on it? We'll explore this in the next chapters of this part of the book.

6.7 Key takeaways

- Asking the right questions of the data is crucial, as some answers may not be revealed without the right queries. The following are good topics to ask about regarding data and corresponding matters around it:

  - Quantity and quality of the data.
  - Models you'll use.
  - Data integration.
  - Expected benefits.
  - Privacy and data security matters.
  - Project ownership.

- Automation uses software bots, AI agents, and ML systems to handle repetitive tasks, adding value through increased efficiency, improved accuracy, cost savings, scalability, and compliance. Automation can be used for back-office operations, customer service, supply chain management, marketing, and manufacturing. However, not all processes can or should be automated, as some may require human interaction.

- The human aspect of automation involves training people to handle changes incurred by automation, ensuring that everyone involved knows what processes are automated and how. This includes providing a heads-up for customer-facing departments when introducing automation.

- A data culture is a collective behavior and belief system that values, practices, and encourages the use of data to improve decision making, affecting not just data workers but the entire organization. Having a healthy data culture can lead to successful data projects, better communication and collaboration, and more effective decision making.

- A strong data culture enables organizations to make more data-driven decisions, understand data as a resource, and foster transparency and accountability. It also makes collaborating with external partners or contractors knowledgeable about data easier.

- A useful taxonomy of data literacy levels is the following:

  - Data novice.
  - Data enthusiast.
  - Knowledge worker.
  - Data expert.
  - Data professional.

- Data analysis supports a data-driven decision rather than opinion or emotion. It involves using data to identify problems, analyze options, and make informed decisions. This approach can provide better decision-making support, confidence, and communication.

- Before adopting a data-driven approach, consider asking yourself key questions such as: Do you have the necessary data? Is analytics sufficient or should you use decision science instead? How can you collect relevant data in the future? Who are the subject matter experts you can consult? How will you store and utilize this information?

SEVEN

What other data can you acquire?

"Questions are the creative acts of intelligence."

Frank King

7.1 Why do you need to get additional data?

In the previous chapter, you learned that you need to think about data going beyond the data you have at hand. To clarify and go deeper, we'll explore the process of getting additional data, starting with the most important question: *Why?* As F. Nietzsche famously wrote, "If you have a strong enough *why*, you can manage any *how*." Although he probably wasn't thinking about data work when he came up with this, this mindset applies to this endeavor too!

Starting from an obvious answer, you may consider what would happen if you don't. You may avoid additional costs and risks, but would you be better off? Chances are that if you don't get this additional data, you can be sure your competitors will. It's not that data beyond your organization is forever available only to you. Data is like natural resources—so many players in the market have access to it, so if they are determined to get it, you can be certain that they will, sooner or later.

What's more, if you are honest with yourself and what your organization needs, you probably have figured out that your existing datasets will likely be insufficient. The data at hand being insufficient may also translate into missing out on signals that are essential in the decisions made based on that data. You cannot act on a weak signal with confidence, but you need to strengthen it before you can take it at face value (and get some real value out of it). This is made possible through many ways, with additional data being the most low-hanging fruit.

Your existing datasets may also have biases that, hopefully, at least one of your data workers has identified and pointed out. In any case, it's rare to find a truly unbiased dataset, and even big tech companies suffer from this issue despite their plethora of resources. Unfortunately, it's not a problem that can easily go away. Nevertheless, with additional data, you can mitigate it and manage it better.

A more subtle reason you may want to get additional data is that you often don't know what you don't know and how it could be useful (or harmful). There are things we don't know that we are aware of (known unknowns) and these aren't so much of an issue. We'll eventually look into them if we remain curious, turning them into something known. What about all the things we don't even know that are out there? They may still be valuable or problematic, and we have no clue. Having access to more data may shed some light on them, making them, at the very least, something we can factor in our risk calculations and incorporate in a SWOT analysis.

7.2 Who could you ask about this?

One of the characteristics of a good data player (who is either a leader or on the path to becoming one) is that they rely on various sources of information during their research. Questions are great, but they can only get you so far. Sometimes, you need to pick up the phone (or launch your favorite VoIP application) and reach out to someone to get to the bottom of a matter. The question that arises then is, "Who are you going to call?" (Hint: it's not Ghostbusters!)

Your data stakeholders are one of the first groups you could talk to and inquire about this matter. This includes the data workers you have in your team, particularly the ones with a broader understanding of your organization's datascape and the world of data in general. These people may be technical, but they are probably business-savvy enough to help you connect the dots between the real world and the data. Also, they may be familiar with particular limitations in your datasets to address through acquiring additional data.

If you have the budget for it, you can also reach out to consultants. These individuals may not be more competent than the ones you already have in your organization, but they are very likely to have a better perspective. This is because they:

- don't owe anyone in your organization anything, so they can speak freely about everything they observe and offer unconventional solutions,
- aren't too immersed in your organization's daily workflow, so they can offer a bird's eye view of the situation,
- are fully aware that unless they add value to your organization, they are not going to get any more revenue from you in the future.

Additionally, your organization is bound to have partners or entities in the industry that you work with collaboratively. These people may also have something to say about additional data and may even have some for you in exchange for insights, or data from your organization's repositories. In any case, that's worth investigating as it can help you increase your options.

Other stakeholders of your organization's data initiatives may also be worth contacting. These may offer you additional insights on what is needed from the business side of things, as well as potential contacts you may want to reach out afterward.

7.3 What are the limitations of the data at hand?

Even though you're bound to get a more accurate view of the specific limitations of the data you currently possess, it's good to be aware of what such limitations may look like.

For starters, no dataset is 100% complete. No matter how many data points you have and how good the performance of the data models you have running on these datasets, there's bound to be room for improvement. This improvement may be in very practical and measurable areas, such as the performance of the predictive models trained on it, or in more subtle areas, like quality, biases, and even missing values. Every dataset may look fine on paper, but you'll realize there are issues once you look at it more closely.

However, the limitations of the data at hand may go beyond the data itself. As other stakeholders may point out, this data may be inadequate for tackling the problems your organization needs to solve. Perhaps the ones you've tackled so far look fine, but what about the others you haven't considered yet? What about problems in other departments? So, the limitations of the data may be a bit relative and only apparent when viewed from this angle.

Beyond that, there is always stuff you and everyone else in your organization haven't thought of yet. These unknown unknowns affect your data's value and express themselves as limitations no one may even be aware of. These may become apparent sometime in the future, manifesting as problems with the data projects.

So, talk to your data workers and anyone involved in the data to learn more about the data's limitations. This is not just one quick chat before lunch but something that may require recurrent meetings, some with multiple stakeholders, to get to the bottom of what you need in terms of data. Otherwise, you will be in a vulnerable position when the time comes to make the corresponding decisions, making you unprepared for what comes next. If you are lucky, you may get some good quality data at a reasonable price, which may not bring you the expected benefits.

7.4 What data streams[9] should you prioritize?

In Figure 7.1, you can get a good idea of your options for data streams that you can acquire, potential sources for them, and even related technologies (e.g., APIs, web scrapers, etc.). Before you decide on this matter, it's good to consider what you might want to prioritize.

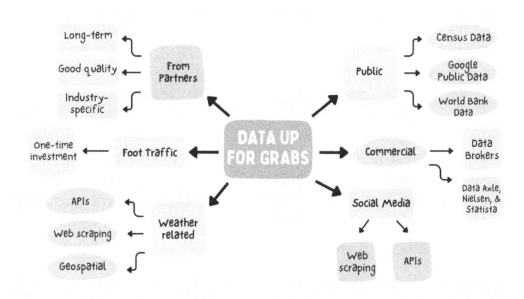

Figure 7.1: Potential data sources for your data projects.

---

[9] This is basically any collection of data, particularly data that is regularly updated or having a temporal element to it. A dataset, on the other hand, is a collection of data that is more static. If you are in the market for new data, you're more likely to be looking for data streams.

A good place to start when getting new data streams is the value-add of each. If you can estimate this well, you can prioritize the ones with the best value-add overall across different data projects. However, remember that this is not set in stone since the value-add may depend on other factors, such as the data workers' ability to integrate and analyze the new data.

Prioritizing the most accessible data streams is another strategy worth considering. This is particularly useful if you are looking into doing a proof-of-concept before investing in a larger form of a particular set of data streams or a more comprehensive selection.

If your data projects are in hot water, you may wish to opt for data streams that are most necessary. These may not always be the best value-add overall, but in the short term, they are what you may need to get these projects to completion.

All in all, deciding which data streams to prioritize depends on the problems you are solving and their severity. So, despite what someone else may say, it's good to take a step back before making such a decision and think about its consequences, both in the short- and long term. Although additional data is bound to add some value, whether or not it's a good ROI in the long run is a different story.

7.5 Can you really trust data that you don't own?

Now that's a good question that some people don't even bother to ask. Somehow, in their naivete, they assume that anything out there in terms of data is benign and valuable. If we apply the same logic when gathering stuff that grows out in the wild, we'll suffer from food poisoning by the end of the week! Fortunately, things in the data world aren't as dramatic, but it doesn't hurt to be cautious.

Chances are that if you are paying for a data stream, it will be vetted to some extent. So, how much you can trust this data depends on the source. You are less likely to have issues with it if it's reliable. If it's some website from some place in some country you have a hard time finding on the map or some website you can only access if you know its URL, you may want to rethink your strategy!

Additionally, check the age of the data. If the age of the data isn't apparent in the data itself, it should be available in the metadata accompanying the data stream.

One way to test the veracity of the new data is to test it against things you already know. Does the new set of variables provide similar results when applied to your data projects? Or does it seem redundant? Let your data workers experiment with it and see what they have to say.

Finally, although it's a viable strategy to expand your data with additional data streams, it's good to remember that there is no substitute for data you own and have full control over. What happens if the data vendors you work with on a new data stream go out of business in five years? What if they decide to raise their prices the next time you need an update on that data stream?

7.6 What about privacy considerations?

Privacy is a very big topic! Still, after having a couple of in-depth chats with a couple of experts in this area, it became clear that this topic is better left to the professionals in that field. Still, it doesn't hurt to tackle it, inspire you to investigate it further, and perhaps talk to such professionals.

We usually address privacy considerations in the metadata of a data stream. However, this is the bare minimum of what to do. This topic will not need our consideration if the data is properly curated. Most people who deal with data have a rudimentary understanding of privacy and how it relates to data work. It's usually only after the CIO or some privacy consultant fiercely reminds them that they need to pay attention to this matter. Metadata is a good starting point, however.

Beyond metadata, something you can easily do to ensure the data remains private is to use some combination of specialized methodologies for this particular purpose. These are *anonymization* and *pseudonymization*. Anonymization is easier and entails removing any fields (variables) containing Personally Identifiable Information (PII). Of course, this isn't good news for anyone who wishes to do something useful with these variables. Pseudonymization offers a compromise in that regard. It helps you cloak the PII in those variables, enabling your data workers to use them in their models. This isn't as powerful as anonymization since it is possible for someone who's determined enough and has sufficient computing resources to reverse engineer the original data fields, thereby retrieving the PII. Additionally, with today's AI-based systems, it is possible to predict these fields in some cases.

In any case, if privacy is a concern for you and you find that the data at hand, particularly the newly acquired one, is bound to give you a headache, talk to a privacy consultant. This may be an investment that may pay off dividends in ways that are difficult to measure, but may be as real as the threat of data leaks. After all, data may be ones and zeros when processed in a computer, but there are often real people behind those numbers, whose privacy deserves to be respected and protected.

This is a good segue to the next topic in this book, bringing the whole data matter into context. Namely, we'll examine questions and answers around a key part of data work: the professionals involved and the technological tools leveraged in data projects.

7.7 Key takeaways

- Not getting additional data can be costly and risky, as competitors will likely obtain it eventually. Even if your current datasets seem sufficient, they may be insufficient for making informed decisions or identifying important signals.

- Your existing datasets may have biases that can't be easily eliminated, and adding more data can help mitigate these biases and improve decision making. Additionally, additional data can reveal unknown unknowns (things you don't even know exist) that could be valuable or problematic.

- A good data player relies on various sources of information during research and doesn't just rely on questions. This includes reaching out to data stakeholders, such as team members with a broad understanding of your organization's datascape, or external consultants who can offer a fresh perspective.

- The limitations of a dataset may also extend beyond the data itself, considering how it may not be adequate for tackling all organizational problems. Additionally, there may be unknown unknowns that affect the value and reliability of the data, which can only become apparent in the future.

- To avoid being unprepared, it's crucial to engage with data workers and stakeholders to fully understand the limitations of your dataset. This requires ongoing communication and collaboration to identify potential issues and make informed decisions about the data's quality and suitability for specific use cases.

- When considering new data streams, prioritize them based on their value-add across different data projects. Consider factors such as the ability of your team to integrate and analyze the new data. While this isn't set in stone, prioritizing high-value-add data streams can help drive project success.

- If your projects are struggling, consider prioritizing the most necessary data streams to complete them quickly. While these may not be the best value-add overall, they can help get your projects back on track.

Ultimately, deciding which data streams to prioritize depends on the problems you're solving and their severity, so it's essential to think about your decision's short- and long-term consequences.

- Test the veracity of the new data by applying it to your existing projects and seeing if it provides similar results or seems redundant. Also, ensure that the metadata accompanying the data stream is accurate and transparent about the data's age and quality.

- While expanding your data with additional streams can be a viable strategy, remember that there's no substitute for owning and controlling your own data. Consider the risks involved, such as vendor bankruptcy, price increases, or changes in their offerings, and have a backup plan to ensure business continuity.

- While privacy is a complex topic best left to professionals, it's still important to consider privacy implications when acquiring new data streams. Start by looking at the metadata, but remember that this may not be enough to ensure privacy.

- Anonymization and pseudonymization are two specialized methodologies that can help ensure privacy. Anonymization removes personally identifiable information (PII), while pseudonymization cloaks PII, allowing for its use in data models without compromising privacy.

What technologies and professionals will you need?

"Questions are the tools by which we learn."

Ben Shneiderman

8.1 Will you be able to handle the data you need?

That's a good question despite its simplicity. Most people don't ask it, go into the whole new phase of their data initiative unprepared, and suffer all sorts of issues from delays to data integration problems. To answer this question, it's good to take a step back and view what data work involves.

Data work is all about collecting data from various sources (through the relevant database queries as well as for loading data files), processing it, exploring it (that's where the first visuals come in), processing it some more, building models off of it, validating those models, and deriving insights from them. At any point during this process, the data professional may go back to a previous stage and repeat the tasks there. This fairly complicated process gets even more complicated when the data availability increases. Think of it as organizing a bunch of books, periodicals, and other items at a library to find an answer to your research question. Even if you are a trained librarian, you will need time to accomplish this task properly. The more items available, the harder it will be.

Only in the case of data work, the various books and other items aren't all neatly organized in bookshelves, but instead a combination of organized bookshelves, boxes, and items scattered on the floor!

Another thing you may want to consider when incorporating additional data and evaluating your ability to handle it is the scope of the data projects involved. What's their time frame when it comes to predictions? Will other people use them too in the future? What are the acceptable margins of error? You'll need to answer these questions to understand where these projects stand and how the additional data will benefit them. Beyond that, you may also want to explore what additional data projects will need to come about based on the new data and evaluate their expected benefits.

Expertise, outsourcing tasks, and the tech involved are additional topics to consider in answering your original question. The data itself can't do much other than sit there and perhaps inspire some stakeholders. It's the expertise that certain professionals bring to the table that makes it into something useful. This expertise may be already in-house, or may need to be recruited, or perhaps leveraged from external collaborators like consultants.

8.2 What technologies are available?

There are plenty of technologies out there that you can leverage in data projects, which we can categorize as either in-house or cloud-based.

In-house technologies are all the equipment and software within your organization for your data workers. These include the following:

- Whatever can run a machine learning or any other kind of data model. A typical example is a workstation with plenty of RAM with a good GPU. You can upgrade it and it's more ergonomic than a laptop. Additionally, the various peripherals can be moved around the organization as needed, making the overall investment more long-term.

- Specialized software for storage and easy access to data. This includes SQL, NoSQL, and graph databases.

- Programming languages like Python and Julia (along with essential packages like scipy, numpy, MLBase.jl, and DecisionTrees.jl), notebooks and IDEs (e.g., Jupyter, Visual Studio Code, and Atom), and big data systems (e.g., Apache Hadoop and Spark).

- Specialized tools for time-series analysis, like InfluxDB, OpenTSDB, and TimescaleDB.

- Technologies like SAP HANA, VoltDB, and GridGain for fast in-memory processing of large datasets.

- Data integration/Extract, Transform, and Load (ETL) tools, such as Talend, Informatica, and Microsoft SSIS.

- Data visualization tools like Tableau (commercial), Power BI (commercial), D3.js, the Matplotlib library in Python, and the Plots.jl library in Julia.

- Other pieces of software depending on what your data professionals require for their work.

Cloud-based technologies are also essential these days and involve specific services on various big tech platforms, enabling your data workers to store, access, and run models and other scripts there. These include the following:

- Amazon Web Services (AWS)
- Microsoft Azure
- Google Cloud Platform (GCP), and
- IBM Cloud.

Finally, there may be other technologies specific to your domain when working with data. These technologies may not be strictly related to analytics. Still, you can leverage them for other processes, such as handling lead information for your sales team (e.g., a CRM system) or accounting data for your corresponding department.

8.3 What about the people operating these technologies?

Data professionals have evolved a lot over the past few decades. Originally, people versed in science worked with computers for their mathematical models. Later, as technology became more accessible, people specialized in different areas started using it. As data-processing software became more readily available, more people started flocking into the field, focusing on its governance (efficient storage and access to data, primarily), analysis (the predecessors of today's data analysts), advanced modeling (mostly data mining), and reporting.

Data mining professionals eventually graduated from their antiquated models and explored better ways to crunch numbers. The advance of technology helped in that, as it was now possible to work with several machines in parallel. This brought about the creation of a new field: data science. Parallel to all this, the scientists who worked with computers using other advanced models explored the possibility of getting machines to do all the hard work for them in a field they called "artificial intelligence." This involved a bunch of different methodologies, one of which is still popular today: artificial neural networks. Although AI evolved in parallel to data science, with a rivalry between AI professionals and ML experts, eventually, there was enough of an intersection between the two fields that some people started doing both. As the software advanced and diversified, certain new data work roles emerged, such as the data visualization expert.

Yet, as the old proverb goes, "The more things change, the more they stay the same!" Despite what they are called today, data workers are still tasked with analyzing data (across different domains and types) to produce something useful for those in charge of the data department. It's still people who are good with computers (at varying levels) and eager to learn new techniques and do something both interesting and useful for their roles. Unlike the data people of the past, however, modern data workers tend to be more business savvy and have significantly better communication skills (at least, that's the expectation).

Regardless of specialty, the main types of data professionals are versatilists, generalists, specialists, and amateurs. Specialists and amateurs are the most common. However, you wouldn't want to hire amateurs on your team, no matter their qualifications. Specialists are better as they tend to go very deep into their area of focus and be very efficient in their work. Generalists may be able to cover different areas, but not as deeply in any of them. These tend to be good for data teams that are still in formation, e.g., in start-ups. Versatilists are those rare individuals who are very good at one thing and able to handle other specialized roles. These are ideal for leadership roles and you can view them as a combination of generalists and specialists. Although it's good to include all types of data professionals in a data team, it's best to opt for versatilists whenever possible, especially if you want a smaller team and wish to use it to its full potential. A versatilist may be harder to find, but it's closer to what some call the "unicorn" data professional.

Data workers can also be classified based on their specialty. In Figure 8.1, you can view the key categories of people you are bound to need for a successful data project. You probably already have some of them, so you can utilize them there. However, depending on your project's sophistication, you will need some additional expertise. In the third part of this book, we'll talk more about AI experts and AI in general.

TECH AND PROS YOU WILL NEED

DATA SILOS

NON-DATA-SAVVY MANAGERS

LACK OF DATA LITERACY

DEVS

DATA-SAVVY MANAGERS

ANALYSTS

DB TECH

DATA ENGINEERS

DATA SCIENTISTS

AI EXPERTS

CLOUD COMPUTING

WHAT YOU PROBABLY HAVE NOW

WHAT YOU ARE BOUND TO NEED

Figure 8.1: Tech and professionals you will need for your data projects. Even if you don't have all of them, at least make sure you have at least five different types, starting with the ones in the intersection.

8.4 What about the rapid rate of change in tech?

That's a troublesome matter, but it is one you cannot ignore if you want your data team to remain relevant in the future. Data work has evolved and continues to evolve. This is what drives the change in technology. Naturally, the changes in tech also bring about changes in data work. The change in tech pushes changes in data work, too. Some of the latest observable trends in data work involve all of the following:

- **AI augmentation**. This is using AI on top of someone's work to improve scope and/or efficiency. When leveraged properly, modern AI can accomplish that, effectively acting as a force multiplier in your organization's workforce of knowledge workers.

- **Deep learning**. This is the latest evolutionary stage of artificial neural networks. These highly sophisticated AI-based models can process all kinds of data with minimal data processing beforehand and are very accurate in their predictions (although different types can be used for different tasks beyond predictive analytics).

- **Data storytelling**. This involves explaining the key insights and making the whole project more accessible to everyone else involved.

- **Explainability and transparency**. This involves making the data models easier to understand and tracing their predictions to specific inputs.

- **Responsible AI**. This involves the ethical use of AI systems and their practitioners taking responsibility for them when they fail.

- **X factor gaining more value**. This is something few people note (the *Cognilytica* AI Today podcast[10] team being a notable example) and involves non-technological elements gaining more significance as everything else becomes more accessible to AI.

Evergreen attributes in data workers have always existed and will continue to exist. These are akin to the X factor mentioned previously and involve soft skills like problem-solving, creativity, and communication abilities. How are these relevant to data workers? Well, let's just say that to tackle the complex problems that data work often entails (especially in the more advanced methodologies, like

---

[10] https://www.cognilytica.com/aitoday.

predictive analytics), you can't rely on recipe books and on people who know enough just to follow such recipes.

Some would go so far as to say that creativity and problem-solving may be the next differentiator of data workers, distinguishing the truly capable ones from those relying on AI to accomplish their tasks. Now, the question for you is, can you discern who has these characteristics among the data workers you bring to your team?

8.5 Can AI help in all this?

There is little doubt that AI can be valuable in data work. However, how much so depends on the quality you expect in your data projects. If you just want to go the easy route and use AI for everything, you will have the following issues:

- Lack of transparency
- Risk of being unreliable
- No sense of context and interpretability
- May not always be able to scale well (lack of automation potential)

Additionally, this trend of AI augmentation these days far outweighs any AI system by itself. This means that a human empowered by AI in their work can be more efficient, skillful, and competent than someone not using AI or even an AI system by itself.

Regarding the technology part of data work, there is no doubt that AI can add value as long as you have sufficient data. The one thing an AI-based data model has an edge over conventional models (e.g., most non-AI ones employed in machine learning) is better accuracy. This comes at a computations cost (i.e., they take longer to train) and with a higher demand for data. Put simply, if you don't have enough data, the AI model would be a waste of resources. So, if you are not content with the performance of your data team's models, or you are willing to explore new possibilities in predictive analytics, additional data is a worthwhile option.

Before you start writing checks, however, make sure you are clear about what you want out of it, which people you want to involve in this, what expertise you are willing to pay for, and most importantly, what data you want to use with AI.

8.6 Can you make your data strategy future-proof?

For the final question of this chapter, let's consider what a future-proof data strategy would look like first. This is the strategy that you wouldn't have to change significantly, one that would work even if external circumstances change in the months or years to come. In essence, you and your data team will need to be future-proof if the data strategy will have a chance of being so, too. This may not be easy since being future-proof is no trivial task. And with the way the tech and data world are changing these days, who is to say what the future will hold for us?

Technology comes and goes, with even the flashiest systems eventually becoming unappealing and obsolete as new ones emerge. Not too long ago, everyone saw ChatGPT as the best thing ever, and some even took courses and workshops to learn about this exciting new tool. Then newer versions of the AI tool arrived. Who's to say that the same thing won't happen to the latest versions of your tools? However, those skilled in a tool out of vogue may still be useful because they can pick up the skills or know-how required to work with the next cool tool.

One thing that attracts all good data professionals in an organization is a robust data culture. This is also what keeps them relevant and enthusiastic about your organization. Coupled with the right people to make this data culture something tangible, these appear to be the most resilient attributes of a future-proof organization with a chance of a future-proof data strategy that works not just on paper but in practice.

8.7 Key takeaways

- **Data complexity**: Handling new data requires a process that involves collecting, processing, exploring, building models, validating, and deriving insights. This process can become increasingly complicated as the amount of available data grows.

- **Project scope and goals**: Consider the time frame for predictions, potential future use by others, acceptable margins of error, and expected benefits from incorporating additional data into your projects.

- **Expertise, outsourcing, and technology**: Evaluate whether you have in-house expertise to handle the new data or if you need to recruit external collaborators or consultants. Additionally, consider the role of technology in supporting your data work and potential bottlenecks that may arise.

- There are different kinds of tech you need for data projects:

  - **In-house technologies**: This includes equipment and software to use in-house.
  - **Cloud-based technologies**: This includes services on various big tech platforms that enable data workers to store, access, and run models and scripts in the cloud.
  - **Domain-specific technologies**: Depending on the domain or industry, other technologies may be specific to data projects but not necessarily related to analytics.

- **Types of data professionals**: There are four main types of data professionals: versatilists (rare individuals who excel at one thing but can handle other roles), generalists (can cover different areas but not as deeply), specialists (go very deep into their area of focus and are efficient in it), and amateurs (not recommended for teams).

- **Specialties within data work**: Data professionals can be classified based on their specialty, including AI experts, data analysts, data scientists, data visualization experts, and others. These specialties are necessary to successfully complete a data project, and some may require additional expertise depending on the project's sophistication.

- **Tech evolution drives changes in data work**: The rapid pace of technological advancements in areas like AI, deep learning, and data storytelling is driving changes in data work. These trends include AI augmentation, deep learning, data storytelling, explainability and transparency, responsible AI, and the X-factor gaining more value.

- **Evergreen attributes remain essential**: Despite the changing tech landscape, certain soft skills like problem-solving, creativity, and communication abilities remain crucial for data workers. These attributes are necessary for tackling complex problems and differentiating top performers from those relying solely on AI.

- **Evolving requirements for data workers**: As technology advances, the ability to discern which data workers possess these evergreen characteristics becomes increasingly important. This includes identifying individuals with strong problem-solving and creativity skills, which may become the next differentiator of data workers in an AI-driven landscape.

- **Quality matters**: AI can be a valuable aid in data work, but only if you expect high-quality results. Low-quality expectations may lead to a lack of transparency, unreliability, and poor interpretability.

- **AI augmentation is key**: When used wisely, AI can empower humans to be more efficient, skillful, and competent in their work. This trend of AI augmentation far outweighs standalone AI systems.

- **Clear goals and data requirements**: Before investing in AI, clarify your expectations, identify the people involved, determine the expertise needed, and define the data you'll use with AI. Only then can you proceed with a beneficial investment that works for both you and your data workers.

- **Flexibility and adaptation**: A future-proof data strategy requires being flexible and ready to adapt. This means being open to changes in external circumstances and able to pivot when necessary.

NINE

What will this cost?

"The power to question is the basis of all human progress."

Indira Gandhi

9.1 What are the financial aspects of governing data?

The matter of cost is crucial for every organization that respects itself. After all, you are not running a data charity. Data is a potential asset and you want to treat it this way. So, how is all this going to affect your bottom line?

First of all, it's good to realize that even if some data is freely available, the adage that "there is no such thing as a free lunch" holds true in the data world, too. So, even if it's not much, there is a cost to keeping this data stored, organized, and handled properly. In data-speak, we call this governing the data (data governance[11]). As the data you have grows or gets more complex, this cost is bound to grow, too, if this data is to remain accessible.

---

[11] A more comprehensive definition for data governance is the following: a data field that involves organizing, managing, and monitoring the integrity and security of data in an enterprise's system. Its business requirement involves establishing policies and frameworks to facilitate these processes, ensuring that any new or existing data complies with current internal and external regulatory standards (e.g., GDPR, PECR, HIPAA, etc.).

The overall cost of data governance depends on your requirements. In other words, what you want to do with the data. If you just wish to store it safely somewhere, it shouldn't cost you much (the cost of data storage per GB has diminished in the past years and the trend is bound to continue). However, if you wish to harness this data in analytics, AI, and other applications, building pipelines around it, that's a different story. So, it's good to figure out your exact data requirements before putting numbers on the corresponding spreadsheet to assess costs.

Hopefully, the message that came across was that data is an investment rather than a sunken cost. Even if the scope of this investment isn't always properly defined (after all, you can reuse data across projects), data is there to provide value and possibly revenue. As such, treat it carefully because even the best data can expire (i.e., stop being relevant or useful).

A good ballpark estimate for data governance for an organization is around 30-35% of a company's operating revenue, although this can drop significantly with good data practices.[12] This may seem a lot for some organizations, but it is quite reasonable considering how much a data breach might cost (a figure that can go in the millions of USD per breach). The exact figure for your organization will, of course, depend on the infrastructure and people you get involved with in this process.

9.2 What are the costs of new data streams?

When it comes to getting new data streams, there are costs involved, too. Usually, these are recurrent costs since it's rare for a data stream to remain useful forever, so it will probably need to be updated periodically.

---

[12]   Source: https://bluexp.netapp.com/blog/cds-blg-data-governance-cost-savings-what-is-data-governance-costing-your-company (last accessed: July 2024).

Sometimes this cost can be unpredictable, at least in the long term. This all depends on the data vendors, who may continuously increase their pricing. That's one of the key risks involved in the data trade business. After all, the exact cost is subject to the agreement made and this may also vary from month to month, based on supply and demand.

A good estimate is a few cents per GB of data. Sometimes, the cost is in terms of stream-hour. In any case, it also depends on the kind of data you are buying, the time frame, and other factors. Compared to the value this data can bring, it's not that much when analyzed properly. You need to make sure you have the right infrastructure first, of course.

9.3 Is freely available data a real thing?

Despite the adage about free lunch at the beginning of this chapter, there is the possibility of getting data for free these days. This is usually done through a process called web scraping. As the name suggests, it involves scraping a website's content and storing its most relevant parts in a database (or a data file). It's so simple that the author of this book has guided many beginner-level data scientists on how to do just that, mainly by using Python. However, you can use several other programming languages for this purpose.

You need to be aware of a couple of things when doing web scraping. First, ensure that the script you build and run delivers the exact kind of data you need. So, it's common to let it run for a bit, check the data, and then restart. This can be done more than once, depending on the complexity of the website. Additionally, it's good to always put some random delay (usually in seconds) between two consecutive calls to the website's servers. This way, the latter won't think you are a hacker trying to launch a DoS[13] attack and block you. Sometimes, the server

---

[13] Denial of Service. This is a common attack on a website, rendering it useless due to the excessive number of calls to it. It's like if you flood a customer service call center with

may block you regardless, if it figures out what you are doing. That's the risk you must take when doing web scraping. Asking for permission from the site's webmaster beforehand may help deal with this issue preemptively (a good strategy if you plan to get lots of data from that website).

It's also possible to get free data through partnerships. If you have a good relationship with another organization that has data you need, you can come up with an arrangement where you can exchange this data with your own data or some other value preposition that works with them. The good thing about this is that it can strengthen the partnership and foster better collaboration on other verticals.

You can obtain free data from various data repositories, too. This may not be as effective as a way to get good data, but sometimes it's good enough to start a proof-of-concept project. A good example of such data is demographic data. This sort of data is usually well-maintained and updated periodically, so it's not that bad. Other repositories that are uploaded once and then forgotten are a different story. Hopefully, your data professionals will be able to discern what's worth downloading and what's not.

Finally, there is also the option of custom-built datasets developed from scratch. This may be free when it comes to data, but it takes some effort on your part. You may need to figure out a configuration that works well, doesn't break any laws, and is efficient enough to provide you with a decent data stream. Then, you need someone to actually go and collect the data, or set up the equipment for this task and check it periodically. This can involve going somewhere physically or installing a device that can access people's phone signals (as a way to gauge foot

---

robotic callers making it impossible for a legitimate customer to get a free line. Naturally, most webmasters hate it when it happens and go to great lengths to prevent it by discouraging this kind of behavior.

traffic) without messing with their phones. The best part about this strategy is that it's entirely within your control and you don't have to worry about fees that may change over time. As long as you respect the people involved, you should be fine.

9.4 What are the kinds of costs involved in a data project?

Let's now look at the different kinds of costs involved in a data project more closely. First of all, there are infrastructure-related costs. This primarily involves equipment and software. A good estimate for all this is between $50,000 and $100,000 as a one-time investment (for computers, GPUs, and other relevant hardware and software), plus the recurrent fees for cloud usage. The latter depends on the amount of data you work with and the computational intensity of the models you run with them, so it varies greatly from project to project.

Then, there is also the cost of intangible resources, such as data-related ones and training. Even if your data workers are quite knowledgeable, have a budget for their ongoing education (e.g., conferences, courses, workshops, etc.). Additionally, other people in your organization may need to boost their data skills, something that can happen with some training from time to time. Depending on the scope of the project, it can go from $10,000 to several hundred thousand dollars, depending on how much training you plan to provide and to how many people.

Finally, there are the talent and project-related expenses (getting the projects up and running). This also includes potential consultations, external mentoring, etc. Although this type of cost largely depends on the team you plan to have, it can run way into the tens of thousands of dollars.

In Figure 9.1, you can view a summary of all the costs involved in a data project or a data initiative in general. Note that domain-specific costs are not included in this diagram as they are something you need to investigate on your own, and they vary greatly from industry to industry.

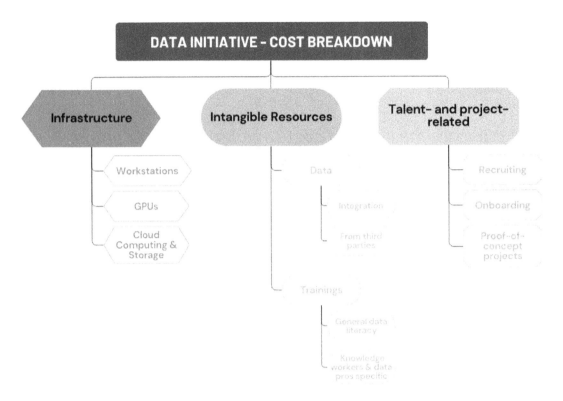

Figure 9.1: Cost breakdown of a data initiative (e.g., a data project). This is just a bare-bones taxonomy of the costs. You can use this as a starting point and flesh it out to make it relevant to your own data initiative.

9.5 What about the human costs when things go awry?

The human cost when things go awry is an important topic that is bound to be a long discussion. Still, it's a valid question since things don't always go according to plan. The human costs usually involve compromised PII or dissatisfaction with a data product. More often than not, these are mutually exclusive and involve two different kinds of people. In the first case, it's people who aren't even aware that you are using their data. These can be customers, employees, or anyone involved in your sales funnel. If you are using their PII and it gets leaked, then this translates into potential lawsuits and serious damage to the organization's brand. In the case of people dissatisfied with a data product, the costs are relatively small, as it's just people who don't like the services involved and feel that their time (and data) is wasted.

In any case, involving a privacy consultant whenever you deal with PII is always good to ensure that the first (and most severe) kind of potential human costs are addressed before they manifest. Additionally, data literacy training can help mitigate the risks involved in both of these two categories. Data security can also help prevent the first kind of issue. After all, PII breaches don't happen because of poor data work but rather because of insufficient data security. The latter involves encryption, key management, various anonymization and pseudonymization methods, etc. Although most data workers aren't experts in these, you can tackle these matters by leveraging a consultant who is also knowledgeable about data and fostering a strong data culture.

9.6 Are there any hidden costs you need to be aware of?

Beyond the monetary and human costs, there are also potential hidden costs involved in a data initiative. These are always there, though often preventable. For example, we already mentioned the cost of lawsuits in the case of privacy compromise. Even if it is preventable to some extent, it's good to be prepared when dealing with sensitive data.

Additionally, there are delays in the delivery of data projects. This is often due to the data not being information-rich or the models taking longer to refine. After all, a data model isn't a magic wand that makes data suddenly useful. Just like every other piece of technology, it takes some fine-tuning before it can be of value. This fine-tuning is hard to put on an accurate time frame and may incur delays, especially when lots of data is involved.

Finally, there may also be other domain-specific hidden costs. These may have to do with the processes involved in the organization, particular protocols, and even the whole pipeline of getting the outputs of the data into a useful state for the users involved. This may even involve specialized equipment, as in the case of manufacturing facilities. Whenever work hazards are involved, there may even be specific compliance matters to address. Yet, even if there are no direct hazards, if your organization is dealing with EU citizens and managing data around them, it must comply with the GDPR legislation. All these situations may have costs that you will have to include in your financial planning.

9.7 Key takeaways

- **Data governance costs**: The cost of storing and governing data is crucial for every organization. While some data may be freely available, there is still a cost associated with keeping it organized and accessible. This cost can grow as the data grows or becomes more complex.

- **Costs depend on requirements**: The overall cost of data governance depends on what you want to do with the data. If you just need to store it safely, costs are relatively low, but if you want to analyze or use it in applications like AI, costs can be higher. It's essential to define your requirements before estimating costs.

- **Cost estimates**: A good ballpark estimate for data governance costs is 30-35% of the organization's operating revenue. This may seem high, but considering the potential cost of a data breach (in the millions), it's a reasonable investment. The exact figure will depend on the infrastructure and personnel involved.

- **Costs of new data streams**: There are recurrent costs to consider when acquiring new data streams, as these data streams typically need periodic updates. Costs can be unpredictable in the long term due to factors like changing vendor pricing. A good estimate is a few cents per GB or stream hour, depending on factors like data type and time frame.

- **Web scraping**: Web scraping involves building a script to scrape content from a website and storing relevant parts in a database. However, be aware that you need to ensure the script delivers the desired data and consider adding random delays between calls to avoid server blocking.

- **Free datasets from repositories and custom-built datasets**: Obtain free data from various repositories, such as demographic data, which may not be perfect but can help with proof-of-concept projects. Alternatively, develop a custom-built dataset from scratch by collecting data yourself, which gives you full control over the process but requires effort and resources.

- **Infrastructure-related costs**: This includes equipment and software expenses, with a one-time investment ranging from $50,000 to $100,000. Recurring cloud usage fees vary depending on the amount of data processed and computational intensity, making it difficult to estimate.

- **Intangible resource costs**: This includes data-related resources and training for employees, with estimates ranging from thousands to hundreds of thousands of dollars, depending on the scope of the project and the number of people needing training. Ongoing education expenses can include conferences, courses, and workshops.

- **Talent and project-related expenses**: These costs involve setting up projects and teams, with estimated expenses ranging from thousands to tens of thousands of dollars. The amount depends on the team's size and requirements for getting the projects running.

TEN

What are the risks and opportunities at play?

"He explained to me with great insistence that every question possessed a power that did not lie in the answer."

Elie Wiesel

10.1 What are the most common risks and opportunities?

In previous chapters, we have examined some of the key risks in data work. However, it would be useful to recap a bit here. One of the main risks is exposure to PII. It's not that someone would do this intentionally, but in this day and age, where data leaks are fairly common, this risk is very real.

Regulatory compliance (and the fines that ensue when this isn't there) is another risk worth considering. With so many laws and regulations in data work, it's easy to neglect something and end up being liable for fines that would be severe for any organization, apart from the big tech companies.

Additionally, in a data project, the ROI may not be what was originally estimated due to delays and other issues that can come about. The presence of stakeholders who don't understand how data works is also a factor that can exasperate this risk.

Related to this is the risk that data may not deliver the value-add expected. Even if it does deliver something, the value-add may not be that significant in the eyes of the user, especially in the long term. For example, a catchy "order" button on your organization's website may result in a relatively successful data project. Yet, users of the website may not respond positively after a while, as they get used to it or find themselves distracted by other eye candy on their browsers.

A final risk is that you may not be able to gain a competitive edge on a data initiative or project because one of your competitors gets there first. This sort of risk may not seem as crucial for a larger organization, but it may be detrimental if it's a small company or a start-up. In any case, it's good to be aware that if you have a good idea for a data product, chances are that someone else in another organization is thinking about the same thing and may have even started working on it.

As far as opportunities are concerned, data work has a few of those, too. For example, a key one is the emerging trends that data work yields. It's easier to navigate a room with the lights on, but it would be foolish to try to do so in the dark when you have the option of illumination. Yet many people navigate the complex landscape of the market without the lights on (i.e., knowing about market trends). Interestingly, understanding where the market is going can be known through intelligent use of data, which is made possible through data work.

Improved efficiencies is a key opportunity too, particularly in processes that haven't been optimized before, are a big plus. Naturally, this involves a lot of advanced methods, but even a simple (yet robust) data model can help that to some extent. The important thing is to identify what can be improved and how data can aid in this improvement, focusing on the cases where these improvements are more accessible.

Cutting down costs is another opportunity involved in working with data. This may be a special case of the previous one, but it deserves its own mention as it's very common. You can potentially cut down costs by analyzing the various waste factors, identifying the ones that are easiest to reduce, and optimizing cash flows by evaluating different alternatives based on data gathered around this matter.

Finally, data-driven innovation is an opportunity that feels like a hidden gem. After all, not everyone can pursue it, while in some industries, it's harder than others. In the era of AI, it's not uncommon to develop novel strategies and products through this technology. And the more data you have available, the better the chances you'll come up with something original.

10.2 How can you model all this in practice?

This is a question prompting for action, and a good follow-up of the previous one. The simplest thing you can do is lay down all the risks and opportunities of a project side-by-side, much like you would do for a pros-and-cons list. If you want to make this a bit more sophisticated, you can add weights to each and calculate to see if the net benefit (sum of weighted opportunities) outweighs the corresponding cost (sum of weighted risks). Ideally, you would also add monetary weights to each item on that list, though this might be challenging in practice.

Alternatively, you can model all this using a SWOT analysis and work with that until the decisions to make become clearer. If you have the resources, you can assemble a data visualization to summarize them properly and perhaps even add weights to each element in this model. Again, you'll need to talk to various people involved and ensure you have all the relevant information before moving forward. We'll talk more about this model later on in the chapter.

At the end of the day, it doesn't matter so much what framework you use. You are fine as long as you consider all the relevant information, model it in a way that makes sense to everyone involved, and come up with a good decision. We focus more on the SWOT analysis in this chapter because it's popular and easy to grasp.

10.3 What is the biggest risk in data work?

Someone would probably ask this question first, as risk is more important for some people when deciding to launch a data initiative. Although the weights of the different risks ultimately depend on your organization and the state of the data available, one thing is riskier than anything else mentioned previously. Namely, it's not doing anything at all!

Asking questions and contemplating about data may seem wise in the short term, but sooner or later, you'll need to take action. The longer you wait, the bigger the risk of your competitors gaining on you or even getting an advantage. This is especially the case if you are in a position where you have room for exploring new possibilities, as in the case of a smaller company or even a start-up. The adage "fail fast," a mantra in the entrepreneur world, holds the essence of a risk-embracing attitude.

Being risk-averse may make sense in certain industries, but it's a very problematic attitude when it comes to data work. Not only are you missing out on great pay-offs through the various opportunities mentioned previously, but you also insulate yourself from the innovation spirit accompanying this kind of risk-taking attitude. You don't have to be reckless (nor should you), but you don't need to be conservative either. As a bonus, the trust you show to your data professionals when you are open to exploring data projects with them is bound to pay off in the long run, both in employee retention and in growth for the people on your data team.

10.4 What is the biggest opportunity in data projects?

Contrary to what evangelists say about data projects and how they can make your organization the best one in its industry, the biggest opportunity has shifted since this advice was relevant. You can still gain a lot from data projects, but it would be hard to gain huge advantages by that alone. So, it's safe to say that the biggest opportunity is to remain relevant as an organization in the 21st century. Naturally, if you go the extra mile and build on the data products, perhaps even find new revenue streams around them, then new opportunities may present themselves.

As relevance often depends on how an organization relates to other players in the market and its customers, staying relevant involves the following:

- Enhanced reputation and credibility (e.g., through responsible use of data and a high level of cybersecurity)

- Talent attraction and retention (e.g., through better evaluation of candidates and employees using relevant metrics and being transparent about it)

- Strategic partnerships and collaborations

- Improved customer experiences (e.g., through personalized services and better customer service)

- Competitive advantage

- Data-driven culture (this point cannot be stressed enough)

When it comes to specific companies that draw value from data work, the following are some good examples:

- **Netflix**. Although its business is primarily entertainment, a lot of its revenue relies on data products like its stellar recommender system.

- **Uber**. It's clear to anyone who has used a car-sharing service like this that without the data products developed on its app, it's not any better than a regular taxi agency.

- **Coca-Cola**. Regardless of whether you enjoy its soda drinks, you would agree that its marketing is one of the most effective. This and its product development, sourcing, distribution, and production decisions are all data-driven.

- **Starbucks**. Through the data gathered from its app and loyalty program, this company leverages data to personalize its marketing, customize its products, and optimize discounts.

- **Amazon**. Despite its humble beginnings as an online book-selling company, Amazon has become a global marketplace for almost any product in a mall or drug store. This is largely due to its data-driven philosophy and the use of data to drive business decisions on all levels.

10.5 How can you decide all this without regrets?

Making decisions is linked to data work but it's not the same. In fact, a whole different field called decision science handles this kind of task.[14] This field borrows from some of the same areas as traditional data work does (statistics, simulation theory, decision trees, etc.). However, no matter what tools you use, deciding on something like a data initiative will carry a certain responsibility that will fall on someone's shoulders. Tools can only help you so much.

If you are the decision maker, you can go the traditional way or apply a more data-driven approach. However, this doesn't mean that you shut yourself in your office and work with a spreadsheet all day. In fact, you should involve other people, ask them insightful questions about the data initiative you need to decide on, take notes, and then ponder on the matter. You can also ask a consultant to pinpoint your various (realistic) options.

---

[14] A good introduction to this topic is *Decision Superhero* by Eric Torkia (Technics Publications).

Then, you can evaluate these options, ideally documenting your thought process through every step. The more objective data you gather about the whole matter, the better. Some may not be black-and-white, but you can explore different scenarios and factor them all in your decision.

If you find that the result of this process isn't convincing enough, you can always revisit previous steps (e.g., talk to other people again with new, more in-depth questions) before you decide. Remember that you don't have to go all in. If the decision involves a large portion of your budget, you can start at a smaller scale and then escalate gradually as the benefits of data work become more apparent.

10.6 How can you SWOT-analyze all this?

Assuming you are at a starting point in your data journey, you can develop strengths, weaknesses, opportunities, and threats based on what we have discussed in the book. Be as comprehensive as possible, and if it's too extensive of a list, reduce the scope of the data initiative. An example of a SWOT analysis based on the starting state of such an initiative appears in Figure 10.1. This diagram also summarizes everything we talked about in this chapter. You can use a similar system to customize the various strengths, weaknesses, opportunities, and threats, of your data initiatives or for individual data projects, as needed.

Naturally, if you have already worked a bit with the data at hand or have at least explored the whole matter in some detail, you can make this list more specific. Also, you can add points that make more sense to your situation and remove ones that aren't that relevant. This diagram is a template to get you started.

SWOT ANALYSIS

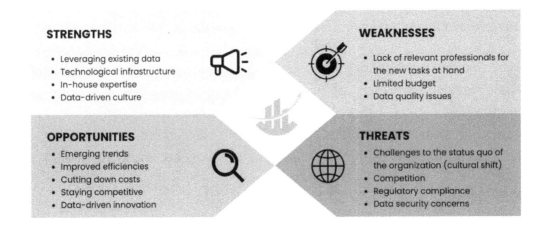

STRENGTHS

- Leveraging existing data
- Technological infrastructure
- In-house expertise
- Data-driven culture

WEAKNESSES

- Lack of relevant professionals for the new tasks at hand
- Limited budget
- Data quality issues

OPPORTUNITIES

- Emerging trends
- Improved efficiencies
- Cutting down costs
- Staying competitive
- Data-driven innovation

THREATS

- Challenges to the status quo of the organization (cultural shift)
- Competition
- Regulatory compliance
- Data security concerns

Figure 10.1: SWOT analysis of a data initiative.

10.7 Key takeaways

- **Some key risks of data work** include:

  - PII being exposed
  - Regulatory compliance (or lack thereof)
  - ROI may not be what was originally estimated
  - Data may not deliver the value-add expected
  - Competition

- **Some key opportunities of data work** are:

  - Emerging trends (in the market)
  - Improved efficiencies
  - Cutting down costs
  - Staying competitive
  - Data-driven innovation

- You can **model the business aspects of a data initiative** by doing one of the following:

  - Lay down all the risks and opportunities of a project in a simple decision model
  - Use a SWOT analysis model
  - Apply some other model that works for you

- The **biggest risk in data work** is not doing anything at all. If you do that, you will lose your competitive edge and follow the trends afterward, with limited benefits.

- The **biggest opportunity in data work** is remaining relevant in the 21st century. This involves several verticals, such as enhanced reputation and credibility, strategic partnerships and collaborations, and talent attraction and retention.

- You can **confidently decide on a data initiative** by talking to other people involved in it (as well as a consultant, if necessary), pinpointing and evaluating your options, documenting everything, and deciding in a data-driven way.

- Conduct a **SWOT analysis** to evaluate your data initiative or project, considering factors discussed earlier in the book, and customize it as needed based on your situation, adding or removing relevant points to involve others and gather input before making decisions.

PART III

What about AI?

"The most serious mistakes are not being made as a result of wrong answers. The true dangerous thing is asking the wrong question."

Peter Drucker

ELEVEN

What does AI have to do with all this? (And what it doesn't.)

"You can be a fool for five minutes if you ask a question. However, you are a fool for a lifetime if you hesitate to ask a question."

Robin S. Sharma

11.1 What is AI anyway?

Many people talk about AI these days, but most of them come from a place of evangelism or consumer mentality. So, let's start with a definition that's grounded more on reality and less on marketing: AI is a field of computer science dealing with the emulation of human intelligence using computer systems and its applications in a variety of domains. The application of AI in data science is noteworthy and an important factor in the field, especially since the 2000s. AI comes in various shapes and forms and these days, it's closely related to machine learning (at least when it comes to data work).

AI is not robots (though there are many robots integrated with AI) and it's not some know-it-all that always has our best interests in mind (at least in principle). AI is not conscious at the time of this writing, and it's not good at everything. Most of the AIs out there are good at one or two things. For example, recently, the publisher of this book used one of Amazon's AI systems to transform various books into audio ones. This same AI may not have been very useful for other tasks, though chances are that for every task that lends itself to automatic processing, there is an AI for it these days.

There are various types of AI systems. The most established ones are data models (deep learning networks we've heard about for years). Additionally, there are language AI systems (Large Language Models, or LLMs), often in the form of chatbots (e.g., Llama, ChatGPT, Gemini, Minstrel, etc.). Some AI systems that usually employ LLMs also specialize in content generation, such as text, images, music/sound, and even videos. Finally, AI systems involve automation, which may even take the form of specialized mobile devices (not smartphones, but more like dedicated AI assistant devices) and other similar gadgets.

It's important to reiterate that AI is not how it is portrayed in sci-fi movies. These films may inspire people and AI system creators, but the technology is far more limited and often requires debugging—much like modern cars are nothing like the cars from sci-fi movies, as they still break down occasionally and require regular maintenance.

In this chapter, we'll explore AI in general, focusing on how it relates to data projects, how to leverage it for provide business value, and say a few things about artificial general intelligence. Note, however, that this book is not a comprehensive guide to AI and that Technics Publications has several other books that cover this subject in more detail. The author wrote such a book project with a fellow data professional.[15]

---

[15] Zacharias Voulgaris and Yunus Bulut, *AI for Data Science: Artificial Intelligence Frameworks and Functionality for Deep Learning, Optimization, and Beyond*, Technics Publications, September 2018. It uses Python and Julia code.

11.2 Why is AI often relevant in a data project?

Let's tackle questions about how AI can be useful for an organization, particularly with data projects. As mentioned previously, the most mature AI systems are related to data models. That's because AI was originally designed for data work (AI back then included other things, too, such as expert systems, fuzzy logic, neuro-fuzzy networks, etc.). So, using AI for data work is aligned with its original purpose.

Additionally, AI is known to thrive on lots of data. Some claim that AI is a good solution to the problem of big data (or perhaps it's the other way around!). In any case, AI systems outperform conventional data models when abundant data is available for training them.

AI ideally handles complex situations and sophisticated problems. You'd often encounter such problems in many data projects, where lots and lots of data points come into play and the signals involved are hard to leverage with conventional data techniques.

We can leverage AI in data projects in various ways. The most common and value-bringing is through DL networks. These are essentially very large artificial neural networks (ANNs) mimicking human brains, designed for data tasks like classification, regression, dimensionality reduction (making the dataset more compact), etc. There are more types of DL networks today than ever before, so if there is a process in data work that you need done, chances are there is a specialized DL network designed for this particular task.

AI is a powerful educational/research tool, too. Today, AI is used to learn new things or organize a research project. A medical research doctor recommended one of the most useful online AI systems the author has used. Although the tool[16] is not only for research, many researchers use it for their work, and it's also very useful for all kinds of educational purposes that traditionally require a search engine. That's not to say that this is the best one out there, but it's a good starting point should you wish to use AI for this purpose and are tired of conventional search engines and the information overload they often yield.

11.3 What are the main pitfalls and limitations of AI?

AI is not without its problems, something that's good to be aware of when engaging in projects relying on it. For instance, over-fitting is a real problem sometimes, not just for AI-based models but for conventional ones that exhibit a certain level of sophistication. This issue occurs when a model is overly focused on the data it has been trained on and cannot generalize properly. Unless you give an overfit model something that very closely resembles its training data, it won't be able to make heads or tails out of it and is bound to make inaccurate predictions.

Over-reliance on AI is another issue when we leverage AI excessively. This translates into not using any other kinds of models, even if there are use cases fit for them. We seem to forget the adage that also applies to data work, "Keep it simple, silly" (the KISS rule). The over-reliance on AI may be more subtle than this as more and more AI systems enter our workflow, making it a problem not just for the data worker but also for anyone getting into the habit of using AI applications daily.

---

[16] perplexity.ai (also exists as an app for the two main operating systems for mobile devices). Note, however, that just like any other AI tool out there, it has its set of limitations. Exercising critical thinking when using it is strongly advised.

AI's most notable pitfall in data work is its lack of interpretability. AI models are referred to as black boxes due to their opaque nature, where it's extremely difficult, if not impossible, to understand how they arrive at the conclusions they do. On top of that, when they have some biases built-in, it's hard to pinpoint them (and fix them) until it's too late. This makes refining AI models very challenging, even for big tech companies.

Lack of accountability is another issue that involves AI. This one, however, is not AI's fault, per se. As automation becomes more commonplace, finding someone responsible for what is happening in a data pipeline (or any other business workflow that leverages AI heavily) becomes harder and harder. Can you blame the AI for messing up an order, communicating inaccurate information to a customer via the website's chat feature, or making predictions that derail strategy? If not, then who is to take responsibility for these matters?

The issue of unknown biases in the AI models is a bit more subtle here as they are not even known to us. The model may not discriminate against one or the other minority group, but it may have a combination of features working together as a bias. For example, it may yield results that imply that customers from a certain postal code, who are also middle-aged and fluent in a certain language, are better than others when it comes to sales. This may have some truth to it, but what if that's an empirical rule the system has discovered because most of the company's customers are in this particular bucket? Does it mean customers from a different postal code aren't worth paying attention to? This bias may not cause customers to become vocal about it (most may not even notice), but this only makes the problem harder to pinpoint and resolve.

11.4 How do GenAI, Automation, and DL factor in?

Let's now zero in more to specific AI technologies and how they play a role. First of all, Generative AI (aka GenAI) can also be useful in data projects. This technology, mainly related to LLMs, involves artificial creativity, a popular aspect of modern AI. GenAI can be useful in different verticals, such as the following:

- Developing text based on a given prompt. This text can be used as a supplement to existing data to enhance the corresponding datasets.

- Developing numeric data based on existing such data. This can be useful if you have sufficient numeric data to augment the corresponding dataset, especially in cases where specific classes are under-represented in the original data.

- Developing visual data based on either text or existing image data. Depending on your application, you may need visual data to improve your existing datasets.

As for automation, it has been used extensively for several years. Lately, however, it has received a major upgrade by integrating it with AI. Automation can now not just help certain tasks be carried out more efficiently by outsourcing them to computers, but it can potentially intelligently do all that. A lot of sound engineering, traditionally done by experts in this field who have studied the subject, can be done through an AI-powered automation process. Many professional podcasts these days employ such a technique.

As for deep learning (DL), this is a big one which deserves to be reiterated and explained more. DL can often be used with minimal pre-processing in the data, making it very efficient. Naturally, if your data workers take the time to pre-process themselves, this can usually improve the quality of these data models. We can also use DL in combination with other data processes. So, you can use a DL network to develop some very information-rich variables and then feed them to some other model to make predictions. Alternatively, you can combine two different kinds of DL systems to create something new. For example, a text-related DL (or even an LLM) and an image-related one, to develop an AI that can create captions for images or images based on given prompts (which is basically what some GenAI systems do).

Mixing and matching different AI systems isn't limited to DL, however. In fact, you can do that with many AIs as long as there is a good understanding of the data involved. Naturally, such combinations of systems need to be explored properly, involving at least one AI expert. However, the possibility is there and AI can be a value-add in this way too.

11.5 To what capacity can AI be leveraged?

Leverage AI for tasks that are either work-intensive, time-consuming, or mundane. At the same time, you can keep a human in the loop as the bearer of responsibility and as a steward of sorts, ensuring everything functions as expected.

That same person can also act as a coordinator. Even in sci-fi films, someone needs to make certain decisions and coordinate the various computing resources available. So, the idea of a fully automated workspace is not near reality. It's important to highlight the decision-making aspect here, too. Even the most sophisticated AI is not designed to make decisions for us. However, it can support our decisions and provide a more objective framework for the decision-maker.

Finally, the human agent should also lead a data project. Having a person with some data skills who can jump into it when something goes wrong is a big plus. After all, even the best AI systems break down sometimes, and when they do, another AI is unlikely to fix the problem. Besides, the holistic view of the project is still impossible to outsource to an AI unless it's a particularly trivial project. In this case, you are still better off assigning it to a person as a way for them to practice and eventually level up.

So, with this out of the way, let's look at the various verticals to leverage AI. This is possible through the four main areas described already: automation, content generation, chatbots, and advanced analytics. A summary of these appears in Figure 11.1.

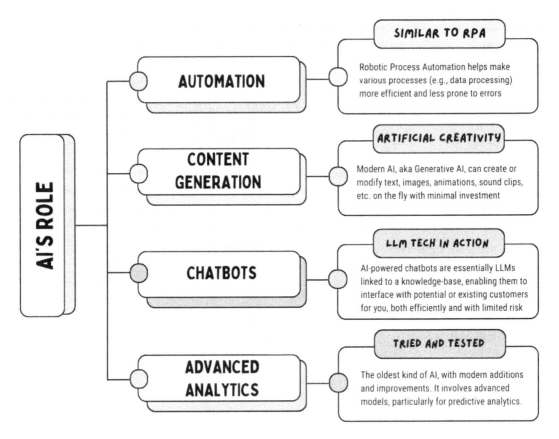

Figure 11.1: AI's role in a data initiative. It's important to remember that regardless of how AI is applied, keeping some human in the loop is always good.

11.6 What about Artificial General Intelligence (AGI)?

AGI has been talked about more than any other type of AI and has sparked a lot of interest in scientific research and science fiction.[17] This kind of AI involves a system that can perform a wide variety of tasks at a level equal to or greater than that of a human who is good at these tasks. For example, an AGI could produce a good quality video based on a prompt, summarize text, process your podcast recording, create catchy marketing copy, draw up an aesthetically-pleasing image, and do math like Wolfram Alpha.[18] In essence, a functional AGI system would be closer to what is shown as AI in sci-fi movies, minus the special effects and the extra drama.

However, whether AGI is possible with existing technology or data supply is unclear. Some speculate that quantum computers could be leveraged for this kind of technology, alongside all the data a computer could get its hands on. Yet, even with state-of-the-art quantum computing, AGI remains an elusive goal.

If AGI were feasible (not just theoretically possible, but technologically doable), it would be a huge value-add. Some theorize that it would be able to tackle unsolved problems that could help the world at large, such as coming up with more efficient engines, new energy sources, and even solutions to biomedical problems. It would be useful in every department of an organization, possibly being a truly unprecedented force multiplier. However, the presence of such a technology is bound to fundamentally change society, so it would be difficult to look at small-scale applications like this one.

---

[17] The author of this book has also written a novel on this topic: "I, AGI: The Adventures of an Advanced Artificial Intelligence" (available on Amazon).

[18] This is the go-to AI for anything Mathematics-related, developed by one of the most creative scientists/mathematicians/businesspeople of our generation. It's accessible at https://www.wolframalpha.com.

Nevertheless, even if AGI were available, it's still unclear if it would be a good replacement for human workers. After all, people are used to dealing with people, so even if you had access to an all-powerful AI system, you might still want to talk to someone if you have a problem that requires the human touch. Organizations like those in manufacturing, telecoms, and other industries with limited customer-facing roles might be a better place to deploy an AGI system. However, it's unlikely to make people obsolete because even in a world where you could print or 3-D print something using an AI system, there is still bound to be demand for artisan products and services, just like human-made paintings and music are still in demand today. Besides, AGI may not be able to resolve the biggest challenge of all: human collaboration, particularly on higher levels. So, it's best not to look at AGI as a panacea but rather as an inspiring possibility that can drive progress in the AI field.

11.7 Key takeaways

- **AI is a field of computer science** that deals with emulating human intelligence using computer systems and its applications across various domains, including data science.

- **AI is not robots or conscious beings;** it's not good at everything but rather excels at specific tasks. Different types of AI systems exist, such as data models (deep learning networks), language AI systems (LLMs), content generation AI, and automation AI.

- AI can be useful for data projects by leveraging its **ability to thrive on large amounts of data**. It excels at handling complex situations and sophisticated problems that involve many data points, making it a powerful tool for tasks like classification, regression, and dimensionality reduction.

- AI can also be used as an **educational and research too**l, helping users learn new things or organize their work. While many online AI systems are available, some of the most useful ones are designed specifically for these purposes, providing a starting point for those looking to move beyond traditional search engines.

- The **key potential problems with AI** in data projects are:

  - **Over-fitting**. Data model cannot generalize well.
  - **Over-reliance on AI**. We depend on AI too much for our work.
  - **Lack of interpretability**. AI models are like black boxes.
  - **Unknown biases**. AI models may conceal very subtle biases that we may be unable to discover and resolve.

- **AI can be a value-add** in a data project through the following ways**:**

  - **Generative AI (GenAI)**: A type of artificial intelligence that involves creative processes, such as generating text, numeric data, or visual data. GenAI can enhance datasets, develop new data, and improve existing ones.
  - **Automation**: It has been upgraded by integrating it with AI, allowing for intelligent automation to perform tasks efficiently and accurately, such as sound engineering or podcast editing.
  - **Deep Learning (DL)**: A powerful AI technology that can process data with minimal pre-processing, making it efficient. Use DL alone or with other AI systems to develop new models, improve predictions, or create entirely new AI applications.
  - **Mixing and matching different AI systems**: The possibility exists to combine multiple AI systems to create something new and valuable. This requires a good understanding of the data involved and the expertise of at least one AI specialist.

- **AI and human involvement**: AI can complete tasks that are work-intensive, time-consuming, or mundane, with a human agent acting as the bearer of responsibility, coordinator, and decision-maker. Even sophisticated AI systems aren't designed to make decisions independently.

- **Human expertise essential**: A human lead is necessary for data projects, especially when issues arise. While AI can be useful in supporting decisions, it's incapable of fixing its breakdowns or providing a holistic view of the project. Assigning trivial tasks to humans allows them to practice and improve their skills.

- **AI application verticals**: Leverage in various areas, including automation, content generation, chatbots, and advanced analytics.

- **AGI is** a system that can perform various tasks at a level equal to or greater than a human expert. Examples include producing high-quality videos, summarizing text, and performing complex math calculations.

TWELVE

When would you want to get AI involved in a data project?

"Questions are the key to knowledge, and answers are the door to understanding."

Unknown

12.1 Isn't it a no-brainer?

Sometimes, the simplest questions are the hardest to answer and the most important ones to explore. Of course, sometimes the answer isn't as clear-cut as expected. It's not an either-or kind of situation, after all. You can have successful data projects even without leveraging AI. And even for a project that does leverage AI, you might not rely on it 100% either. So, involving AI in a data project isn't as trivial as it may appear.

Instead of trying to give you a yes-or-no response, this chapter will explore the topic in depth from different angles, giving you the tools to come up with your own answer. An answer like this is far more useful than anything you can look up in a book, a search engine, or even an AI system.

On a fairly basic level, where you look at quantifiable things, you can evaluate the relevance of AI in a data project using a set of criteria and adding them up in some meaningful way. An example of such a system is that of Figure 12.1. Note that this is just a starting point to help you gauge if AI makes sense or not. This, however, is just a heuristic to get your mind thinking about the matter and preparing itself for the decision. Even though heuristics play an important role in data work and AI itself, they are not to be taken at face value.

WHEN TO GET AI INVOLVED

What you have	+1	0	-1
Lots of data	○		
Complex problem	○		
A knowledge base	○		
Qualitative data		○	
Unclear ideas on its value-add			○
Untrained data workers			○

Figure 12.1: Getting AI involved in a data project. Adding up all the points you gather from the set of criteria on the first column you can get a score between -2 and 3. This is just a heuristic which you can interpret as follows: any score from 1 or higher means AI is appropriate. Anything below that means that it's not. The higher the score, the better suited AI is for your data project.

To get a more nuanced view of the matter, we'll explore additional questions that you may need to ask, such as what kind of AI is most suitable, how you would start, what KPIs to use, what steps you can take to make AI more useful, and even things like when you should give up on an AI project that's not going so well. No matter what your AI-enthused data professionals might say, whether you involve AI or not in a data project is a business decision. Are you ready to go beyond what all data professionals know about AI and view it more holistically?

12.2 What kind of AI suits your project best?

Naturally, if you want to get AI involved in a data project, you need to figure out the kind of AI you need to use. Just like not all data is made equal, AI systems differ significantly both in how they are built and in how they are a value-add to an organization.

If you have a standard data problem that you are tackling (e.g., predicting the sales of a product or a product line for the next quarter), you ought to look into deep learning. This is particularly the case if your problem involves a lot of variables with complex relationships that may take your data workers a long time to untangle. You can start with a basic DL network (a Multi-Level Perceptron, or MLP for short) and then look into specific architectures that may be more suitable. For instance, if you are looking into a time series analysis, you should go for a recurrent neural network (RNN), while if you are dealing with images or videos, a convolutional neural network (CNN) would be better.

If your project involves a lot of text or if you have a knowledge base you wish to utilize, then an LLM would be your best bet. This is also the case if you are looking into content generation as part of your data endeavor. Which kind of LLM you use is another story, but there is no clear winner at this time. It's worth remembering that there are LLMs that are pretty decent even if they run on a single computer (ideally one with a GPU), so you don't necessarily need to pay for the online ones. Also, most of the LLMs you find on a website dedicated to leveraging them as their main feature will likely collect any data you share with them. So, where exactly you are on the trade-off spectrum between efficiency and privacy will determine what kind of LLM you utilize.

As mentioned before, automation-related AIs would be ideal for improving efficiencies and the programmatic handling of mundane tasks. Many companies offer this as a service (e.g., Zapier), but you can also develop your own. Tools like Fabric (not the Microsoft one) are great for "reducing friction" when using AI, enabling its users to summon the power of an AI system as part of their pipeline without even having to go on a browser.

AI-powered chatbots are a great option if you are looking to interact with users for Q&A or basic queries. However, these chatbots don't have to be only for your (potential) customers since you can have specialized ones to facilitate internal processes and business operations. Chatbots are a very user-friendly interface for LLMs, but they can still incorporate the logic you put in beforehand. So, the LLM takes care of the words part and the scripts handle everything else. The programming logic of a chatbot doesn't require much expertise these days, but if you have an expert in this sort of work, you may be able to make a more sophisticated chatbot that will also be safer for your organization.

Naturally, if your data project involves a more complex scenario, you may want to consider a combination. It's best to break it down into specific modules, each corresponding to an individual AI system, if possible, to avoid getting overwhelmed. This way, you'll be able to monitor progress better and troubleshoot the system more effectively.

12.3 How would you start?

You can (and should) launch a proof-of-concept project when spearheading an AI-related initiative. This way, you can mitigate any risks and ensure that there will be an adequate value-add from the data project. The PoC doesn't need to be trivial, but its scope needs to be limited and there should be a cap on its resources.

If you use AI for analytics, you can start using a simpler model (e.g., a random forest or another ensemble model that doesn't require too much prep work). This way, you can establish a baseline and gauge later how much better the DL model is and whether it's worth the extra effort. If the baseline is quite high, the added benefit will be relatively low, and you may not pursue an AI solution for this project unless this marginal improvement is a value-add for you.

You can also deploy LLMs locally whenever possible. These are LLMs that run on your machines instead of on the cloud. If you have computers with GPUs, these AI systems can run even better. As long as the LLMs you want to run locally aren't too big (in terms of parameters and, therefore, computing resources needed), they should be able to work using one of the following platforms:

- Ollama[19]
- LM Studio[20]
- Pieces for Developers[21]
- LLM script in Python[22]
- Hugging Face Transformers[23]

Should your data project involve chatbots, you can start with a basic chatbot, namely a no-code solution, to explore the possibility and familiarize yourself and your team with chatbots. Naturally, you may want to go for a custom-made solution afterward. Still, the no-code solution may be a good baseline and help

---

[19] Installation instructions: https://www.theregister.com/2024/03/17/ai_pc_local_llm (last accessed: May 2024).

[20] Official site: https://lmstudio.ai (last accessed: May 2024).

[21] Official site: https://code.pieces.app/blog/how-to-run-an-llm-locally-with-pieces (last accessed: May 2024).

[22] Code repository: https://github.com/onlyphantom/llm-python (last accessed: June 2024).

[23] Hugging Dace is an online platform but it can work even offline as long as you have downloaded the LLM model(s) first.

you at least get the basic interface down before assigning developers to this project.

When it comes to analytics, you may want to start with basic deep learning networks before exploring more sophisticated ones or combinations. You can create these easily by training them (locally). Once you are content with their value-add, you can look into migrating the whole setup to the cloud. You may even start in the cloud from the beginning if you are confident with your AI project or don't want to invest in hardware.

12.4 What KPIs would you use?

KPIs are essential in any project as they are a glimpse of how it's faring. Although they are, in essence, heuristics, they are usually very useful ones. When acknowledged properly, they can lead to a good understanding of the project's status and points of potential improvement.

When embarking on an AI project as part of a data initiative (particularly one that involves predictive analytics), you will need to familiarize yourself and leverage various KPIs related to the models themselves. These include the following:

- **Accuracy/F1 score/MSE for the model at hand**. Although these are three different metrics, knowing them is important so that when a data professional reports on how an AI model is faring, you can understand them better. Accuracy and F1 score are used for classification and you can think of them as percentages since they take values between 0 and 1, with higher values being better. MSE (mean square error) is a standard metric for regression scenarios. It can take any positive values, and the lower they are, the better.

- **Model Training Time**. This involves how long it takes for a model to learn enough from the data to generalize and make predictions accurately. Naturally, you'd want this to be small.

- **Computational resources**. This includes the model's computing power to train, the memory it requires, and the storage space it needs.

Beyond these KPIs, there are other ones that are more general or high-level and involve the project overall. These include:

- ROI
- Customer satisfaction
- Time-to-Insight. This involves how much time is needed before you get some insights from the application of the AI system.
- Cost savings

All of the KPIs mentioned previously are useful in their own way. However, it's also important to remember that some factors that cannot be measured are also good to keep in mind. Things like overall confidence in the system, reliability, and a sense of trust in the technology involved. You can manage these better by attaining a certain level of data literacy and domain knowledge on AI.

12.5 What steps can you take to make AI a better value-add?

Naturally, we can always improve AI. Even the state-of-the-art AI available to the world is an iteration of the product that the corresponding companies constantly develop and refine. So, how can you make the AI you use a better asset for your organization?

For starters, you can begin the data project with clear objectives about what it should achieve and how AI would be an intricate part of it. Leverage AI to yield a competitive edge, even if using more conventional data models and methods. At the same time, make sure that your expectations are reasonable and that you have the right people to get the job done.

Additionally, you can ensure that the data used is sound. Many AI projects fail because the stakeholders aren't on the same page regarding the data part, which is far more important than people think. If you have pondered the stuff covered here and hopefully done some research, this point may seem obvious to you. Yet, it doesn't hurt to reiterate it and ensure that everyone involved knows the importance of ample and good-quality data.

What's more, you can ensure there are no biases in the results to the extent possible. This is a blind spot of AI, and if you could mitigate them even a little, it would make for a better AI system. Leveraging your most experienced data professionals (not AI experts necessarily) would be a good tactic.

Finally, you can consider whether transparency is important to the project. Surely, everyone enjoys some transparency in their data models, but if it's not essential for the particular use case, you may be able to do without it. Otherwise, you may want to explore a different solution, perhaps some machine learning model that offers a certain level of transparency.

12.6 When should you give up on an AI project?

When it's clear that an AI project cannot deliver what it set out to accomplish due to technological or data-related limitations, you may want to pull the plug. Be sure to explore what you can salvage from it first. Certain code scripts can be recycled and used in other data projects. Also, the learning experience of your data workers is always a plus.

Additionally, if the project starts getting too expensive, beyond the original budget, you may want to reconsider its status. After all, even if the project finishes, its ROI is bound to be low or negative, so quitting while you are ahead would be wise.

What's more, if the project starts creating issues you cannot resolve, that might be a good time to put an end to it. This doesn't have to be dramatic, like the AI claiming independence and starting a revolution! Even if the system yields bad results, damaging your customer relationships or your organization's brand, that's enough reason to cease the project altogether. AI-powered chatbots are more prone to this kind of situation.

Beyond these, other scenarios may be such that stopping an AI project is the best course of action. Although these may not happen often, it's good to think about them beforehand and prepare for those eventualities. Much like a fire plan is always good to have, even if the chances of an office fire aren't that high, having an exit strategy for an AI project is always wise.

12.7 Key takeaways

- The decision of whether to involve AI in a data project is not as simple as it seems and requires considering various criteria to evaluate its relevance (e.g., amount of data available, the complexity of the problem tackled, whether you have a knowledge base or not, how clear an idea you have about AI's value-add, and how trained your data workers are). Use a heuristic approach to gauge if AI makes sense, but don't take it as the final answer.

- Depending on the problem, you should explore specific kinds of AI. Namely:

  - If you have a lot of variables with complex relationships among them, use a deep learning network.
  - If you are working with text, utilize a knowledge base, or are looking into content generation, use LLMs.
  - If you are looking into improved efficiencies, use Automation-related AI.
  - If you are looking into interacting with users for Q&A or basic queries, use AI-powered chatbots.
  - If dealing with more complex scenarios, use a combination of these AIs.

- You can start an AI-related data project by doing the following:

  o A PoC project.
  o Work with simpler models when it comes to analytics to use as a baseline.
  o Leverage a native LLM whenever possible.
  o Utilize a basic chatbot (no-code solution) to explore the possibility if your project involves this kind of AI.
  o Train basic DL networks before exploring more sophisticated ones or combinations of them.

- Some commonly used KPIs for an AI project include:

  o Accuracy/F1 score/MSE for the model at hand.
  o Model Training Time.
  o Computational resources.
  o ROI.
  o Customer/User satisfaction.
  o Time-to-Insight.
  o Cost savings.

- To improve AI performance and make it a better asset for your organization, set clear objectives, ensure high-quality data, eliminate biases, and consider the importance of transparency in your project's results.

- You may want to give up on an AI project when:

  o It cannot deliver what it set out to accomplish.
  o It starts getting too expensive (over budget).
  o It starts creating issues you cannot resolve.

Where can you find AI pros who add the most value?

Recruiting AI Professionals

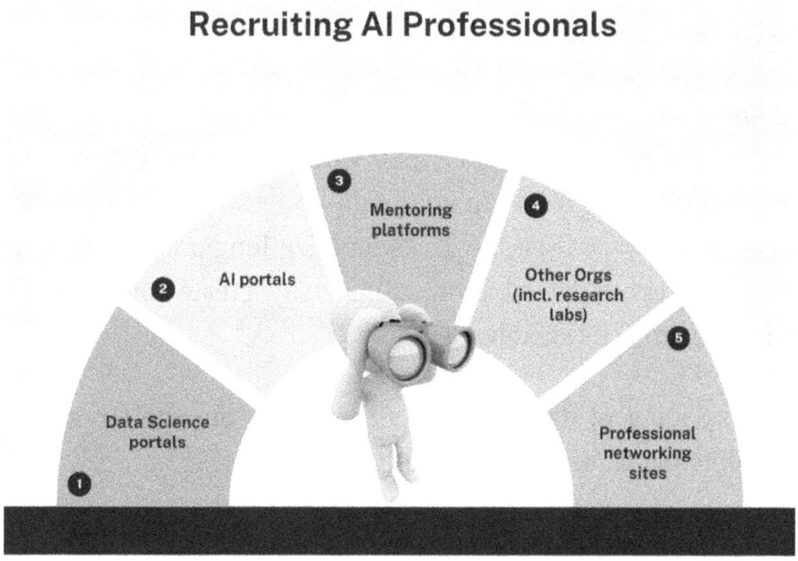

Figure 13.1: Recruiting AI professionals for a data project. As for the value they can bring to the table, that's a whole different discussion. You can start the journey of exploration involved through this chapter.

13.1 What qualifications does an AI professional need?

A good AI professional is like a versatilist in the data science field: very rare and valuable. Unlike what a recruiter may think, such a professional isn't someone with X years of AI experience or knows frameworks Y and Z. The author knows someone with over a decade of AI expertise. However, he has no connection with modern AI technologies or how to use them in an organization. Additionally, some AI pros are very familiar with the popular AI frameworks but don't know enough about data work to add value through these tools. Would such persons be considered good AI professionals? Probably not.

A good AI professional is someone with solid know-how of various DL systems. Such a person is familiar with the corresponding frameworks (e.g., TensorFlow), their programming libraries (how they are utilized via a programming language), how they work, and possibly how to tweak them to yield the value-add they set out to deliver. It doesn't matter if they know just two or a dozen such frameworks since they are very similar, and knowing one very well enables the AI professional to learn another quickly.

A working knowledge of LLMs is also essential as a qualification. This includes prompt engineering, the LLMs' APIs, their various options, and their limitations. Even if you don't deal with text in your data projects, an LLM can be handy in various ways. At the very least, it can summarize long articles on AI topics and make a complex report the AI professional may create into something more accessible for the project's stakeholders.

A solid understanding of data work is essential for anyone working on a data project, including the AI professional.

As discussed, communication is essential too. Communication skills include both expressing themselves and listening well to what you are saying, by the way. Many tech professionals may be good in just one of these verticals of communications.

A good AI professional should also be able to perform critical thinking. Things are not particularly deterministic when it comes to AI, and, at least in the case of LLMs, the same inputs (prompts) yield different outputs every time. So, the AI pro needs to be able to work around this uncertainty when evaluating the models involved to ensure that they are reliable enough. Otherwise, fiascos like the Tay chatbot from Microsoft that, instead of being the paragon of innovation that its PMs envisioned it, ended up being the most racist and overall rude AI system ever released on social media.

Finally, having a good understanding of AI trends and adapting to the developments of AI technologies is vital for an AI professional. Certain things like DL networks may remain relevant for years, but when it comes to LLMs, things change faster than anything else (which is why no reference to specific versions of LLMs is made in this book).

Sometimes, finding someone with all these qualities within your budget for new hires is impossible. However, knowing them is crucial as you may hire someone promising enough to help them cultivate these qualities over time. The same applies to other data workers you gather for your data initiatives.

13.2 How can you discern between AI pros and wannabes?

Many people are still confused about what the role entails and what makes someone really an AI professional worth bringing on board to your data projects. The plethora of AI wannabes out there only makes things worse, as AI professionals are becoming a minority of all the people involved in the AI field.

When AI professionals talk about AI, they tend to be fairly conservative about their projections and not overpromise. On the other hand, AI wannabes tend to think that AI will solve all of our problems and bring about a utopia of sorts. AI professionals base their views of AI on reality and technical know-how, while AI wannabes base their views on blog posts, evangelical videos, and lectures by futurists. In other words, AI pros are usually more down-to-earth and don't speculate much about the tech, while AI wannabes are the opposite.

13.3 At what point do programming skills come into play?

Programming skills are everywhere in data work. However, in AI work, they are even more pronounced. Some data professionals can get away with little coding, which involves calling some libraries and writing some code here and there to stitch things together. In AI, this won't fly. An AI professional needs to be familiar with different kinds (and levels) of coding while being comfortable with the various AI frameworks like those mentioned previously.

Some of the key programming skills involved in AI work are the following:

- Python – the most widely used programming language in data work in general and has plenty of libraries for AI frameworks, such as Tensorflow and PyTorch.

- Java/C++/C# – these more low-level programming languages are very similar in what they do and enable the development of faster code that's ready to deploy in production.

- Data structures and algorithms – this is an essential piece of know-how for any professional involved in the more technical aspects of data work. It involves understanding how to handle and process data, regardless of the languages used.

- Big data processing – this has to do with storing, querying, transferring, and performing various operations on big data. It involves platforms like Hadoop and Spark.

- ML frameworks – this entails specialized frameworks geared towards machine learning applications. Examples: Scikit-Learn, Hugging Face

Transformers, Keras, MS Cognitive Toolkit (CNTK), LightGBM, XGBsoost, etc.

- Cloud computing – anything related to using the cloud for processing data is under this umbrella term. Most common cloud computing platforms today include MS Azure, Amazon's AWS and similar services, as well as IBM's cloud, among others.

- Containerization involves using frameworks like Kubernetes that make it possible to deploy microprocesses, enabling better efficiency and handling of problems.

- CV libraries – these are specialized programming tools that enable the computer to work with images and videos. CV is a specialized sub-field of AI and it's very popular today. OpenCV is a very popular library in CV, which works with Python, C++, and others.

- OS know-how – being knowledgeable about operating systems, especially Linux-based ones, is very useful, particularly when working on a low-level implementation of an AI system.

- Version control – this involves handling different versions of a program or piece of documentation. It's essential for any programming-related work. A popular program for version control is Git (which is independent of GitHub even if the latter employs Git).

- Other, as needed – depending on the domain or specialization of the data work involving AI, an AI professional may need to be familiar with specific software or frameworks beyond the ones mentioned here.

A good AI professional doesn't need to know all of them, but having at least an idea of them is useful. Ideally, that person would have expertise in most of them, with an emphasis on the programming languages. The specialized know-how like containerization and CV libraries may be more relevant when using microprocesses extensively and image-related data respectively.

Programming comes into play once the project requirements are clearly defined and conventional ML approaches have failed to yield adequate value. Additionally, whenever the organization needs certain levels of accuracy in predictions or the use of a customized AI system, getting your hands dirty with coding is necessary. This shouldn't be an issue for the seasoned AI professional and if that person has the right attitude, they may even enjoy the challenge.

13.4 What's the difference between AI users and AI experts?

Another distinction worth familiarizing yourself with when it comes to AI professionals is that between AI users and AI experts. AI users may be serious professionals who have just delved into AI as consumers but have become more knowledgeable than the average consumer and started tinkering with the systems. They are usually geared towards LLMs and may be adept at getting them to do useful things. These are not the same as the AI wannabes and don't present themselves as AI experts. They just have a penchant for AI systems and make an honest effort to do something useful with them. Anyone who has played around with Llama, Minstrel, (Chat)GPT, or Bloom, and drawn some value out of this experience is an AI user.

AI users and AI experts differ from each other in various ways. The most notable difference is programming expertise. Even if an AI user is knowledgeable in programming, they may not be on par with the AI expert, who is bound to be familiar with more than one programming language.

Additionally, the ability to develop custom AI systems is solely within the AI expert's skillset. The AI user may be knowledgeable in the various flavors of LLMs and be able to tell you which one is better for which task, but they are unlikely to develop a custom AI system. Besides, as we've seen previously, AI systems go beyond LLMs, involving things like deep learning networks, too.

Although some AI users are knowledgeable in Retrieval Augmented Generation (RAG)[24] and may be able to tinker with them, AI experts can usually undertake such an endeavor as part of a data project. Various specialized RAG-related platforms are online, but these are usually commercial products. Knowing how to use them can be useful, but being able to develop one from scratch is a different game altogether.

Finally, the data literacy level often differs significantly between the AI user and the AI expert. The latter is usually at the top tiers of data literacy, where the AI user is closer to the level of a knowledge worker. In any case, this doesn't mean that the AI user is siloed from the professionals in the field. With proper mentoring, training, and experience-gathering, the AI can eventually become a data worker, perhaps even an AI professional one day.

13.5 How can you see beyond the hype of AI?

Seeing beyond the hype that plagues AI (and any other modern technology) requires a somewhat Stoic approach to the subject. In practice, it involves things like:

- Understanding the basics of AI – this is key if you want to truly understand what AI is all about in practice.

---

[24] A RAG is a system that extends the knowledge of an LLM artificially, often through sophisticated prompt engineering, enabling it to be better performing and more useful for dealing with specific knowledge that is important and relevant to the organization. Such knowledge is usually part of a knowledge base and can take various forms.

- Exploring AI applications – this is also essential, especially if you want to make the most of AI in your organization.

- Learning about AI's limitations – this is paramount, as it provides you with a sense of groundedness, which is essential in any kind of data work.

- Analyzing the job market – this is also important for figuring out what kind of roles people with AI expertise can fulfill.

- Considering the societal implications – this is very useful for understanding the effects of this technology and developing a sense of responsibility when using it.

- Staying informed about AI's progress – this is also useful for keeping you up-to-date regarding the field.

- Engaging with diverse perspectives – not everyone agrees about AI, especially today, so exposing yourself to different views enables you to get a more holistic understanding.

- Being aware of AI's potential risks – this is also important since AI is a controversial technology that could easily be abused.

- Embracing skepticism – this is the cornerstone of science and since AI is a scientific field, it's good to treat it accordingly.

- Encouraging responsible AI development – this goes without saying, particularly if you have embraced at least some of the previous points. AI may be risky, but you can contribute to its more beneficial aspects by fostering a more responsible approach.

All these are different facets of the mindset that characterizes down-to-earth thinkers and technologists (even if you don't have all of these, you can still be unaffected by the hype).

13.6 Can you leverage AI professionals for other data work?

Naturally, you may not always have a data project that involves AI. So, what do you do with the AI professionals you have available so that you don't waste their time or the organization's resources? Fortunately, there are ways you can leverage them, at least for the short term.

One of the best areas to allocate an AI professional to data work is as part of the data science team. Whether that person does data storytelling, predictive modeling, or even data pre-processing, it doesn't matter. Chances are that they will be able to do a great job. After all, there is a large overlap between the AI work and the data science one.

AI professionals can also do data engineering work. Depending on how comfortable they are with databases, data lakes, etc., and ETL pipelines, they should be able to add some value to the data engineering aspects of the data projects.

Business intelligence is another area where an AI professional can add value. This is particularly true if that person is a seasoned professional with strong business acumen. By performing anomaly detection or sentiment analysis tasks, they can leverage the insights developed to inform strategic decision making.

An AI professional can also work in predictive maintenance roles. By applying machine learning and natural language processing techniques, they can analyze equipment performance data, predict failures, and develop maintenance schedules to reduce downtime and costs.

R&D work is another vertical related to what an AI can do to add value to a data initiative. Specifically, they can apply their machine learning and NLP expertise to accelerate research in fields such as medicine, finance, or environmental sustainability by analyzing large datasets and identifying patterns.

Compliance monitoring is something else that can occupy an AI professional when they aren't involved in AI work. Namely, they can design monitoring systems to detect anomalies in large datasets related to regulatory compliance (e.g. related to financial transactions, patient data, or supply chain logistics).

13.7 Key takeaways

- The attributes and qualifications of a good AI professional include:

    o   Know-how of various DL systems.
    o   Working knowledge of LLMs (prompt engineering, their APIs, etc.).
    o   Solid understanding of data work.
    o   Good communication skills.
    o   Critical thinking.
    o   Good understanding of AI trends and being able to adapt to them.

- The key differences between AI professionals and AI wannabes are:

    o   AI pros build stuff, AI wannabes talk about stuff.
    o   AI pros are usually down-to-earth and don't speculate about the tech that much.
    o   AI wannabes have little understanding of other kinds of data work.
    o   AI wannabes have completed some bootcamp or read a couple of books and lack any deep understanding of the subject.
    o   AI wannabes don't really care about AI in a meaningful way.

- Programming skills for AI work usually include:

  - Python.
  - Java/C++/C#.
  - Data structures and algorithms.
  - Big data processing.
  - ML frameworks.
  - Cloud computing.
  - Containerization.
  - Computer Vision (CV) libraries.
  - OS know-how.
  - Version control.
  - Other, as needed.

- Programming comes into play once the project's requirements are clearly defined and conventional ML approaches have failed to yield adequate value.

- The differences between AI users and AI experts include the following:

  - Programming expertise.
  - Ability to develop custom AI systems.
  - Ability to build RAGs.
  - Data literacy level.

- To be able to see beyond the hype of AI you need to do (at least some) of the following:

  - Understand the basics of AI.
  - Explore AI applications.
  - Learn about AI's limitations.
  - Analyze the job market.

- Consider the societal implications.
- Stay informed about AI's progress.
- Engage with diverse perspectives.
- Be aware of AI's potential risks.
- Embrace skepticism.
- Encourage responsible AI development.

- You can leverage AI professionals for other types of data work, for example:

  - Data science work (best option).
  - Data engineering work, to some extent.
  - Business intelligence.
  - Predictive maintenance.
  - R&D work.
  - Compliance monitoring.
  - Other kinds of data work until finding a replacement.

FOURTEEN

What kind of information can AI handle for you?

"You'll know her more by your questions than by her answers."

Jerry Spinelli

14.1 What are the kinds of information in a data project?

In Chapter 2, we briefly saw the different types of data you may have in your organization and how it can be useful as a potential asset through data work. Here, we'll do the same for information as a superset, examining how suitable AI might be for it. After all, more isn't always better, and as much as we've praised diversity in data, this diversity may not always be a good thing when it comes to information.

Let's start with the more basic aspects of data models and AI systems: structured data. This kind of data is abundant in databases, spreadsheets, and tables in various documents. Anything like that is great for data models of all types, including AI-based ones. However, you may need to vet such data for quality and relevance to the problems.

Text data is another kind of information that we often deal with. This is on the blurry line between data and information since it's something we often process ourselves through our mental faculties. However, modern AI systems, particularly LLMs, seem to be very good at this, too, with exceptional progress being made since AI-powered chat became mainstream. You can analyze text data in various ways, with AI systems being one of the best.

When it comes to unstructured data, things aren't that black-and-white. Depending on how it is, it may or may not be suitable for AI. Although much of it is text data, which is generally compatible with AI, other kinds of unstructured data are different. Take webpages, for instance. Not all AI can work with them, especially if they have a lot of programming code on them (usually JavaScript). Log files are another example. AI can potentially work with them, but some pre-processing work may be required to make such a data project successful. Beyond these examples, there are other ones, such as sensor data, social media posts, audio files, videos, emails, and images, many of which are fine to tackle with AI. Still, others may require additional work (e.g., sensor data, which is often too convoluted and requires special data transformations before it reveals its secrets, even if it can still be useful in its raw form).

Multimedia data, in particular, is a case where AI can work well if paired with the appropriate DL system. You can't just shove a video into one of the modern AI systems (which are mostly LLMs) and expect anything useful to come out. It is the same with audio files. However, you can process these files and extract the transcript of any language in them, converting it into text (with a special DL network). Then, you can take that text file and analyze it either with an LLM or some DL network (performing NLP). As for image data, you can feed that directly to one of the more advanced LLMs, along with any text clarifying what you need. Still, not all LLMs can handle multimedia files, and sometimes, it's better to break down a task into sub-tasks before getting AI involved.

Regardless of what information you are dealing with and the types of data, it's important to remember that you'll need large quantities of data when embarking on a project involving AI. This data is essential for training the models. However, if the models are already trained (by some other organization that offers them as a service), you don't need much data. That's why many software packages based on AI are so popular today. If you were to build something like this from scratch as a custom AI for your particular use cases, you would need ample data for it to work well.

Figure 14.1 summarizes this topic.

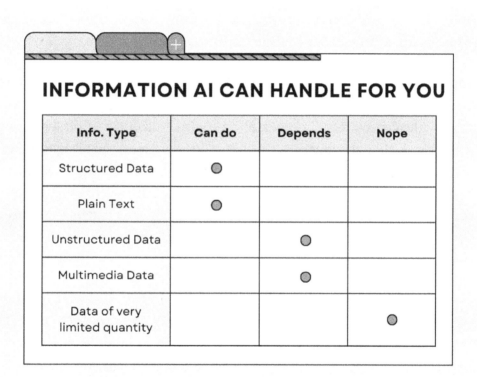

Figure 14.1: Information AI can handle for you. As with any data project, it's good to always consider the quality of the information.

14.2 What's the deal with prompts and prompt engineering?

Prompts have been all the rage since LLMs became commercially available through the freemium model their companies offer. Their popularity increased once open-source alternatives entered the game, making LLMs an easily accessible option to AI without compromising the privacy that the original alternatives entailed. In essence, prompts are the stuff you give to the LLM as an input, simple as that. What's not simple is how an LLM processes those inputs. In fact, we may never know this until we dissect an LLM or have a long conversation with the engineers who created it.

So, we can view an LLM as a black box. What we know about it is limited to what we give it as an input and what we get from it as an output. Fortunately, both are in a human language, so it should be easily understood.

Prompts are very useful if you work with LLMs as they are the data they process and directly linked to the output the LLMs yield. Naturally, the LLMs tend to get creative with their outputs, but they always weave them based on the prompts they receive. Unlike the more responsible of us, they never admit ignorance, so sometimes they make up stuff (aka, they hallucinate), but it's always based on the prompts. However, if you as a user of an LLM are knowledgeable about the topic, you can spot when an LLM is hallucinating, and with carefully engineered prompts, you can get to the truth of the matter (to the extent the LLM knows it, of course).

However, it's important to remember that different prompts may work differently for different LLMs. This makes sense if you consider that each LLM is a different model, even if they all share some similarities in terms of architecture and at least some of the algorithms involved in training them. Yet, the data used in training them may be different or processed differently. So, a prompt that works well with Llama, for example, may be less potent when applied to Minstrel, Gemini, or some other LLM, and vice versa. Also, the same prompt may give slightly different results when applied to the same LLM. This is due to the stochastic nature of LLMs. Also, many LLMs use context based on previous inputs and outputs. So, the LLM may change its mind once you clarify the topic and put it in the right state.

Generally, it's best to keep track of the prompt that works well for you. Some people go so far as to create spreadsheets where they note down the prompts and the responses they got using them for the LLM they used. By carefully evaluating the responses, you can gradually develop a sense of what works and what doesn't. Naturally, this can be time-consuming, so some people specialize in this sort of work. Although not officially recognized as part of AI work, many people know what prompts deliver the best results for a given LLM and can fashion such prompts for different use cases. These people are called prompt engineers.

14.3 What are the AI limitations in handling data, information, and knowledge?

That's a question everyone ought to be asking when using AI or having an AI project planned. As mentioned previously, AI is not a panacea, and it has its limitations.

When it comes to data, AI may not be able to make the most of it if the data has biases or weak signals. Although an AI model can unearth signals that other data models cannot, it cannot find something that's not there. Also, the biases are like colors, and just like every other data model, an AI tends to be color-blind! So, it's very important to be aware that even if you have tons of data, biased data leads to biased responses.

As for information, AI may not always be able to learn information very well, especially if it's conflicting with other information it is trained on. A lack of understanding of how the world works also affects how it deals with information (particularly for LLMs). Unlike people, AI doesn't have common sense, so it may not always understand the subtleties of our reality. Nevertheless, the latest AI models find workarounds on this issue due to their deeper understanding of the information they are fed in the form of text and images.

Knowledge is another area where AI may have limitations, too. If the knowledge is somewhat structured, as in the case of a knowledge graph, everything should be fine. However, if it is disorganized and split across different files, often of a different type, it may not understand it well enough to do something useful. It will still parse them, but what it gets out of them may be questionable. Human supervision and curation are paramount in this kind of use case.

Naturally, there may be more limitations that don't fit into these categories. However, it's good to discern whether these are actual limitations of the technology or if it's something related to how it's used. The latter should be solvable, while the former may be beyond your control. It may still be solved in future iterations of the AI systems, but not within the time frame of your data projects.

14.4 Can you overcome AI's limitations? If so, how?

These good follow-up questions prove not just one's healthy sense of curiosity but also that of tenacity and intelligence. Even if not all the limitations can be overcome, the fact that they can be addressed makes a big difference.

Regarding the data-related limitations, some prep work before using it with the AI model can mitigate the issue. This involves data wrangling and using particular heuristics to gauge the biases. Then, with various specialized techniques (e.g., intelligent data synthesis), the data can be made more balanced, making the biases less of a problem. Note that this is often an iterative process that's hard to automate, so every data worker involved must understand the data deeply.

When it comes to information, some curation of it can go a long way. Additionally, working with the corresponding data can be very helpful, ensuring that any text and images that go into the training set are solid. When deep learning networks are involved, it's not uncommon to add some noise to the data, just enough to help make the AI work a bit harder and generalize better.

In the knowledge domain of AI, proper management of this knowledge and modeling it in a way that makes sense to the AI can be a great first step. This isn't as simple as it sounds, however, especially if this knowledge lives in silos or a large variety of forms. However, it can be done gradually, yielding incremental benefits to the AI system. The Pareto principle can be a good heuristic for navigating this process.

Naturally, there are other ways to deal with AI's issues regarding data, information, and knowledge. This can be viewed as an opportunity to hone your creativity and those of your AI professionals and other data workers. After all, compared to the challenges big companies face regarding AI, these are relatively simple and, most of the time, solvable.

14.5 Diamonds are forever, but can we say the same for an AI system?

Now that's a question for the ages! Although the answer may seem apparent, it's worth digging more into the topic.

Clearly, just like everything else in the tech world, AI too has an expiration date, in the sense that it may not be particularly useful after that (or that it may not justify the resource usage it requires to operate). This may not be something you'd know beforehand, and chances are that no one involved in this technology knows for sure, apart from the manufacturers in some cases.

Additionally, AI systems, especially those dealing with predictive analytics, often require maintenance due to issues like data drift, just like other data models. This is something you can monitor and know as soon as it occurs. This way, you can take action as soon as the problem manifests and either replace the AI model or retrain it. Nowadays, there are ways to do this with some level of automation, so it's not a huge issue.

As new AI systems emerge all the time, making previous ones quickly obsolete, what seems like a good AI system today may be irrelevant in a couple of years. Quantized versions of LLMs[25] are the first to be replaced (by other quantized LLMs) as they tend to be weaker. However, if you are working with LLMs on time-critical projects, chances are that you are using the normal LLMs, even if you have to lease them from the LLM platforms where they live.

Once invented, an AGI is a potential exception to this obsolescence cycle of AI systems. Such a system could keep itself relevant through self-maintenance and constant updates. Some theorize that it might even be able to improve itself, making it better over time. However, since there is no AGI out there at the moment, this is just a theoretical remark to bring about awareness of the bigger picture of the AI world.

14.6 How can you customize an AI system for your knowledge base?

If you have a knowledge base,[26] you may want to use it through its incorporation with an AI system. There are two main ways to go about it: building such a system from scratch or refining an existing AI system (particularly an LLM).

---

[25] These are the more light-weight versions of the LLMs that are designed to run on single computers or even mobile devices. A typical quantized LLM these days has 7-8 billion parameters and oftentimes doesn't require a GPU to run (although the presence of a GPU can greatly improve its performance).

[26] According to the TechTarget site (last accessed in June 2024), a knowledge base is "a machine-readable resource for the dissemination of information, generally online or with the capacity to be put online. Knowledge bases are an integral component of knowledge management systems. They are used to optimize information collection and information organization and retrieval."

If you were to venture such a project from scratch, you could do that through the following process:

1. Defining the scope and goals

2. Selecting the right AI technology

3. Preparing your data

4. Developing a taxonomy or ontology (this is something you may need to get a data architect involved in)

5. Defining entities and relationships (again, the data modeler would be very handy for this task)

6. Training the AI model

7. Tuning hyper-parameters and adjusting performance metrics (these are technical details that every data professional leverages to optimize the model)

8. Validating and evaluating the AI system

9. Refining and iterating

It's not uncommon for the first few steps of the process to take up the most time as it's a tough problem to solve. Also, training the AI model is bound to be time-consuming, depending on the size of the knowledge graph involved.

Should you attempt this venture using a pre-trained LLM as a basis, this is the process you would follow:

1. Information Retrieval. This involves training an LLM to index your document collection, allowing for efficient querying and retrieval of relevant documents based on user input (e.g., search terms).

2. Document Classification. Here, you'd use LLMs to classify documents into categories such as topics, genres, or sentiment analysis.

3. Named Entity Recognition (NER). This step involves training an LLM to identify named entities (e.g., people organizations locations) within your documents, allowing for effective extraction of key information.

4. Summarization. Utilizing LLMs to generate summaries of long documents or articles, helping employees quickly grasp the essential points without having to read the entire document, is what this task entails.

5. Question Answering. Here, you'd train an LLM to answer specific questions based on your document collection.

6. Document Analysis. This step involves leveraging LLMs for sentiment analysis topic modeling or entity co-occurrence analysis to gain insights into the content of your documents.

7. Content Generation. Use LLMs to generate new content based on patterns learned from your existing document collection.

8. Language Translation. This optional step entails training an LLM to translate documents into different languages, expanding the reach of your organization's content and enabling global communication.

9. Text Classification for Compliance. This is an important step that involves data privacy. Here, you'd utilize LLMs to classify documents based on regulatory compliance requirements (e.g., GDPR and HIPAA).

10. Knowledge Graph Construction. This final step entails leveraging LLMs to construct a knowledge graph representing the relationships between entities mentioned in your document collection.

An alternative approach, which is somewhat simpler, involves using RAGs instead. These are built on top of LLMs but don't require much low-level work. In the case of a RAG, the process would be as follows;

1. Ingesting the knowledge base content into a vector store allows for efficient semantic search and retrieval.

2. Designing a prompt template that allows the LLM to access the retrieved knowledge during inference.

3. Tuning various aspects like prompt engineering, hyper-parameter tuning, and filtering of retrieved results to optimize the performance of the RAG-powered system.

Whatever you decide to do to leverage your knowledge base, know that you have options. You don't have to reinvent the wheel (unless your project has very specific requirements that involve a brand new design). In any case, an AI can help you leverage your knowledge base and make the whole thing searchable easily and efficiently, all while keeping your sensitive information under wraps.

14.7 Key takeaways

- The **different kinds of information** (loosely speaking) **good for AI** are:

    o Structured data.
    o Text data.
    o Unstructured data (depending on how it is).
    o Multimedia data (with the appropriate DL system).
    o Across all data types, large quantities of data.

- **Prompts and prompt engineering are very important**, when it comes to LLMs:

  - Prompts: the stuff you give to the LLM as an input.
  - Very useful if you work with LLMs.
  - Different prompts may work differently for different LLMs.
  - Best to keep track of the prompts that work well for you.

- **There are several limitations to AI when it comes to handling data, information, and knowledge**. For example, if there are lots of biases or the signal is weak, the available data may not play well with the AI models used.

- **You can overcome some of these limitations** by pre-processing the data at hand, curating the information involved, and organizing knowledge in forms that AI can better understand.

- **Every AI system is bound to have an expiration date**, though you can sometimes work on it to ensure it stays relevant longer.

- **You can customize an AI system for your knowledge base** by developing an AI from scratch or refining an existing one (usually an LLM), e.g., through a RAG configuration.

FIFTEEN

What kind of investment does AI entail? Is it all worth it?

> *"The art of questioning is the most powerful tool you have."*

Unknown

15.1 How does AI add value to you?

Returning to the initial questions in this book, it's good to look into the value-add matter from an AI lens. After all, no matter how promising AI technology is, what's the point of examining it if it doesn't add enough value to your organization?

First, clarifying your business objectives and how they link to AI is best. Are they something that you can accomplish through other data technologies? Which ones would you prioritize among those objectives? Answer these questions before creating an AI project to meet these needs.

Additionally, you may want to explore what specific data projects you are planning to have that involve AI. As we saw in previous chapters, not every data project is best tackled with AI (even if the temptation to use this technology is strong). If you can handle the project without AI, this might be preferable as it's bound to be more affordable and possibly quicker.

What's more, it's good to look into what features or products you envision involving AI. Maybe you have a chatbot feature in your mind, which would clearly be a good AI application. Or maybe you need to get some automation in your sales funnel, which could be done through AI (at least in part).

Beyond data-related work, you may want to explore what information or knowledge-related tasks you plan to accomplish using AI. Maybe you have a lot of Q&A on your site that you wish to make accessible to your visitors through a chatbot, or perhaps you have a collection of regulation-related documents that your knowledge workers need to be aware of. You need to have a knowledge base they can query. In any case, these sorts of scenarios lend themselves to AI systems.

Finally, examine how these AI-related matters impact the bottom line. Unlike certain institutions, you may not have big grants to fund your AI projects. So, having a clear idea of the cost will make it easier to spearhead these projects and translate them into something your organization's CFO would understand.

15.2 What kind of AI will you use?

Let's now explore the different AI systems you may leverage in a data project, assigning monetary costs to them. Note that these are not absolute figures and are more like guidelines to enable back-of-the-envelope calculations for the projects involved.

For the deep learning AIs, the most common ones in analytics work, the cost of such an investment starts at about $200/month (when using cloud computing). However, this doesn't include the additional costs of data acquisition, pre-processing, and governance.

If LLMs run natively, the cost is north of $20K/month for a single instance (we are talking about regular-sized LLMs here, not the quantized ones, which are good for proof-of-concept projects mainly). Should you opt for a pay-as-you-go solution, this would amount to about $200/month.

Regarding chatbots, custom-made ones will cost $5K/month at a bare minimum, with complex projects going up to $100K/month. Pay-as-you-go solutions are far more affordable, with many free options (primarily for basic functionality, useful in proof-of-concept projects).

For RAG systems developed in a customized way, 2-3 engineers would be required to develop one. Beyond that, there will be operational costs that will depend on the platform used. These costs can be substantial for certain sophisticated models like those by OpenAI.

Automation-related AI systems can also be pricey and require 2-3 engineers to implement from scratch. GPU costs will be high too with a good ballpark figure of $10K or so for a good-quality GPU. Operational costs will be on top of all that and depend on the platforms used.

Naturally, as you scale your AI project, these costs will change. However, in such a scenario, you may be able to negotiate better deals with the AI platforms and mitigate costs this way.

15.3 How would you go about it to minimize risk?

As with every project, an AI project entails a certain level of risk. Fortunately, at least some of it can be managed and dealt with, leading to more successful projects.

You can get some good AI professionals to work on your AI projects. The temptation to get someone on the cheap will always be there, but if you invest in quality and growth potential, you'll be doing yourself and the organization a favor. After all, it's unlikely that AI will become irrelevant any time soon, so investing in good AI people is key to long-term success.

Another thing you can do is start small and expand as you see fit. You don't need to get everything at once, be it the people for your AI team, all the infrastructure, or all the data. Start with what you have, expand gradually, and remain flexible. As the technology evolves, you will probably adjust your AI strategy anyway.

Additionally, you can avoid investing in state-of-the-art equipment. Even a decent GPU can boost the performance of an AI system. Avoid getting the cheapest one, though, as they may not be resellable, reliable, or easy to maintain. The same goes for the models used, at least regarding LLMs. Even the humble open-source models out there, such as Llama and Minstrel, have a lot to offer, so don't limit yourself to the big brands only.

Planning carefully and being ready to adapt to changes in the market is always a good idea for all kinds of tech projects. As the market can be very volatile, it's good to adapt to it instead of sticking to rigid plans and stale expectations.

What's more, you can consider all facets of AI work instead of just the ones everyone else thinks about (see Figure 15.1 for details). Beyond the more data-related aspects of an AI project, other ones are almost as important. For example, the R&D (for long-term AI initiatives), the integration and adoption (which we covered briefly in the earlier chapters), and the cyber-security dimension are all worth considering when embarking on your AI journey.

Finally, you can explore partnership options with other organizations that tackle AI projects or with AI platforms. Through such high-level relationships, you may be able to make strides without having to develop everything in-house. We have already seen how such partnerships can be mutually beneficial regarding data, but their benefits extend to other aspects of data projects, including AI.

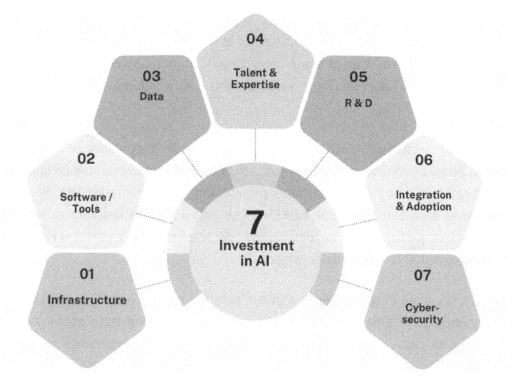

Figure 15.1: Different facets of Investment in AI for a data initiative. Although the value of each will depend on the projects at hand, it's good to address all of them whenever possible.

15.4 What kind of results are you expecting?

This is a crucial matter, as your expectations must align with reality. Many projects fail because management and engineers are not on the same page regarding what's possible and how to meet the projects' objectives.

You can start by clarifying the specific deliverables of the AI projects in terms of technologies, products, revenue streams, etc. Like any other data project, an AI project needs to have specific requirements that its people will fulfill. A simple Gannt chart may not be enough, plus you need to consider other uses of the systems built beyond the projects at hand.

Scalability is another important matter linked to the AI project results. Simple chatbots (the ones that are free of charge or have a very low price tag) don't scale very well. So, if you expect many users to utilize your AI system, you need to plan accordingly. Otherwise, you will have bad UX, which may compromise the whole project.

We already mentioned briefly how data projects can be interconnected somehow. An AI project is bound to have a strong effect on them. However, the technology leveraged in it is bound to affect other projects dealing with similar data. So, plan to harness an LLM. This same LLM may be useful for text analytics in another data project, perhaps even for developing unit tests and other useful scripts that may be essential for all kinds of projects.

Finally, it's good to remember that things may not go as planned. In such cases, it's good to have a backup plan. Can you salvage anything from an AI project that fails to deliver the expected results? Apart from the experience you gain (which will always be there), what other benefits from it can you gather that may at least help you with other AI projects or data projects in general?

15.5 What are other considerations when investing in AI?

Beyond all the stuff we've discussed regarding investing in AI, there are also a few points worth considering for a more holistic understanding.

First of all, AI is highly unstable, as any new technological field is in its first stages. This doesn't mean it may implode at any moment, but there is a high uncertainty surrounding it. That's to be expected, especially since there are so many players in the AI arena these days, many of which are competing for the next big thing, whatever that is. If, for example, tomorrow OpenAI announces a new kind of LLM that can perform all kinds of data and do so better, this may be a game-changer. Or if Meta comes up with a new version of llama that can be quantized so that it can exhibit adequate performance for a normal LLM, this may make online LLMs a far less attractive option.

Additionally, it's good to remember that not everyone can deliver what's possible. AI has a lot of real possibilities in its current state, but not every AI professional or team can bring them about. Maybe the data isn't there (a very common situation!), or the infrastructure is lacking. So, if organization X can do so-and-so with AI, it doesn't mean everyone else can too.

Moreover, not everyone is on the same page about what is possible. Some people speculate that AI can do wonders, akin to what others talk about in their sci-fi books (even if those books are sold as "technical" or "non-fiction" in general). Others have more conservative views. The truth is usually somewhere in between those extremes. It's good to always remember that.

Ethics is also a concern, though not a strict limitation. So, depending on how ethical you are in the use of technology, this may affect what you can do with it. However, we strongly recommend avoiding abusing it as the repercussions may hinder your future rewards, at the very least.

The ROI of an AI project may not be what the salespeople of an AI-based platform promise you. The latter just want to make a sale, and many may not be fully aware of your circumstances. So, no matter what they say to you, always check with your AI professionals before committing to a deal that may not be as beneficial to your organization.

It's best to listen to people with skin in the game rather than futurists and evangelists of AI. The latter may not be fully aware of AI's technical aspects or the data's limitations. They tend to approach the topic from an ideas perspective, which is more idealistic than pragmatic. Yet, when implementing these ideas, things may be very different. That's why it's engineers usually drive this technology rather than sci-fi enthusiasts.

Finally, it's important to consider AI safety. This is a big topic that is more suitable for a whole different book. Lately, more and more people, both from the

AI technology world and other areas of society, are expressing their views about the urgency and importance of this matter. In no unclear terms, they state that the potential threat of AI abuse is akin to that of a nuclear war, so it's not a matter to take lightly. There are also many regulations around AI safety, such as the AI Act from the EU, though these seem inadequate to address this matter. In any case, AI safety concerns everyone and anyone using AI, even for a small-scale project, is a stakeholder on this important matter.

15.6 What's the bottom line when it comes to AI?

First of all, AI is a useful technology but not a panacea of any kind (unless some AI platform develops and releases an AGI tomorrow, in which case this position will need to be revisited!). However, how you utilize it depends on how well you organize the projects involving it, ensuring that you have all the data you need and the people to work the models effectively and efficiently.

What's more, the AI investment landscape involves a lot of facets, some of which may not be so obvious (e.g., those mentioned in Figure 15.1 previously). Although data plays a crucial role in it, other matters, such as R&D and cybersecurity, are often neglected. This leads to a relatively lopsided approach to AI that may be good for short-term profits but not for long-term benefits.

Moreover, whether AI projects are a worthwhile investment should be examined case-by-case. Even if the AI evangelists never get tired of praising the technology and how it's evolving rapidly, how it's adding value is a very relative matter and depends on many factors, such as management, infrastructure, and the nature of the problem tackled.

Additionally, AI has potential as a force multiplier but may not be a plug-and-play solution. For AI to yield real benefits that are both measurable in terms of ROI and sustainability, we need to do a lot of prep work. From organizing functional AI-related teams to developing the right data culture to picking use cases that are manageable and fairly predictable in their time frames, making AI work is a nuanced matter.

Finally, AI has a lot to offer in analytics and other data-related endeavors when handled properly and when good professionals are involved. It's not enough to download the latest AI library or subscribe to a state-of-the-art LLM platform to get an AI-based analytics project off the ground. Sometimes, you may even need to provide some training to the people involved, and more often than not, you may need to involve more conventional technologies. You can think of AI as a powerful SUV you use to go to some isolated hiking/biking path. It may get you most of the way there, but you may still get off it and start cycling or walking to reach your final destination.

15.7 Key takeaways

- The AI value-add should be the primary focus of any AI project. This entails questions like:

  - What are your business objectives and how are they linked to AI?
  - What specific data projects are you planning to have that involve AI?
  - What particular features or products do you envision that involve AI?
  - What information or knowledge-related tasks do you plan to accomplish using AI?
  - How do all these impact the bottom line?

- Different AI systems have different costs attached to them. It's important to be clear about what you need and be prepared for the costs these technologies incur. Scalability is bound to affect these costs, too.

- You can mitigate risks related to an AI project through the following strategies:

- Get good AI professionals to work on your AI projects.
- Start small and expand as you see fit.
- Avoid investing in state-of-the-art equipment. Even a decent GPU can boost the performance of an AI system.
- Plan carefully and be ready to adapt to changes in the market.
- Consider all facets of AI work.
- Explore partnership options.

- Having clear ideas about the results you expect from an AI project is key. This involves questions like:

  - What are the specific deliverables of the AI projects in terms of technologies, products, revenue streams, etc?
  - Is any of that scalable?
  - How does this affect other data projects?
  - Is there a backup plan?

- Some useful considerations when investing in AI as a technology for a data project are:

  - The field is highly unstable, as any new technological field at its first stages.
  - Not everyone can deliver what's possible.
  - Not everyone is on the same page as to what is possible.
  - Ethics are a concern though not a strict limitation.
  - The ROI may not be what the salespeople of AI-based platforms promise you.
  - Best to listen to people who have skin in the game rather than futurists and evangelists of AI.
  - The matter of AI safety is of paramount importance and everyone involved in AI partakes in it.

- The bottom line when it comes to AI in data work can be summarized thus:

  - AI is useful but not a panacea.
  - The AI investment landscape involves a lot of facets, some of which may not be so obvious.
  - Whether AI projects are a worthwhile investment is something to examine on a case-by-case basis.
  - The potential of AI as a force multiplier is there, but it may not be a plug-and-play solution.
  - AI has a lot to offer in analytics and other data-related endeavors when handled properly and when good professionals are involved.

What now?

"The important thing is not to stop questioning."

Albert Einstein

That's a good question! One that everyone enjoys asking to appear engaged or interested. Yet, despite it being commonplace, it's still useful and likely to incite action. For starters, you can always read your notes on the book (or stuff you may have highlighted) and ponder the topic more. If you are so inclined, you can even write something based on that to include in your next newsletter or a blog post (if you do that, remember to include a reference to this book so that others can benefit from it, too).

Once you have assimilated this information and feel compelled or at least somewhat motivated, to take action, you can start exploring various data-related processes in your organization that benefit from this new-found understanding. It doesn't have to be drastic, but even including data-related discussions in your weekly meetings with your team, mentors, supervisors, etc., is a good step.

If you are in a leadership position in your organization, you can take the opportunity to start developing a *data culture*. Even if this involves just helping everyone be unafraid of data-related terms and see the whole matter as a potentially beneficial thing rather than yet-another-thing-they-have-to-learn, it's still a plus. Big changes take time and a cultural shift may take a while to accomplish. However, it's much easier if you are in a position of influence rather than a regular knowledge worker.

Additionally, you can start exploring new data projects to launch after examining their feasibility and value-add potential. Not everything may be right for the present moment, but it doesn't hurt to have them in mind. Even if you launch just one or two of these projects in the next quarter, it's still better than nothing. At the very least, it will be an educational experience and something that you can leverage in the future.

Moreover, you can also explore the questions listed in Appendix A and start using them in your day-to-day work. There are no answers given for these questions, but there is some explanation of the rationale behind each one. This isn't comprehensive, but these questions can be a good starting point. Perhaps you can add more rows to that list as you develop your questioning skills. In any case, pondering on these questions is good practice and can help you engage with the topic of data and its leveraging in a practical and potentially valuable way.

The most important thing you can do, however, is more long-term. It involves developing a questioning mindset when it comes to data (see Appendix B for a simple template for this). Not in a critical way, but more like something from a place of genuine curiosity and interest. Ideally, this should come organically, but you shouldn't hesitate to provide it if it needs a push. The Einstein quote at the beginning of this section can be a good inspiration for that. In this quote, Einstein didn't mention that questioning keeps your mind young. It seems that how we think may be correlated to our physical age, but that's not always the case, and it definitely doesn't have to be like that. Just like the 80-year-old retiree who remains active through walking and gardening is an inspiration to us all for staying fit, regardless of our age, so can the questioning mindset that most great thinkers maintained until their late years inspire us to remain young in how we think.

Developing a questioning mindset is also a powerful tool for communication and collaboration. Think about this for a moment. Who would you enjoy working with, a know-it-all who sounds like a chatbot out of control or someone who includes plenty of meaningful questions in your interactions? Just like you'd probably opt for someone exhibiting some curiosity around you, others are bound to feel the same way. Few people are attracted to managers who are too much inside their heads. Yet, everyone appreciates being asked their view on a topic, especially if it's something they have put considerable effort into, such as their work.

Naturally, asking questions is as valuable as the quest for the answers to these questions. It makes sense to pursue these answers, regardless of the questions, and seek to learn. Otherwise, there is little value in just pondering the questions themselves, even if it's better than passively ingesting information from the web. When you come across potential answers, it's also valuable to question them. Are the sources reliable enough? What biases could they have, be they conscious or unconscious? Are these answers applicable to you? Questioning the answers doesn't necessarily mean doubting everything you come across. It's more like the healthy skepticism every scientist has (or at least aspires to have). This skepticism isn't limited to people of science, however. It's something we all need to have, at the very least, to shield ourselves from low-veracity information and insulate ourselves from the hype of new data technologies.

Mentoring plays a paramount role in this whole endeavor. Whether you are the mentor or the mentee, you have a lot to gain from such a process. Sometimes, explaining something to someone, especially someone who knows how to ask good questions, helps you learn it better and view it from angles you never considered. Additionally, being on the other side of the table enables you to practice asking good questions and pursuing answers, with the mentor guiding you and helping you dissolve any misunderstandings and misconceptions you may have. As a bonus, you may get some actionable information from all this and save you significant amounts of time and effort. Yet, the biggest bonus is the long-term benefit of such a process: keeping your mind open and cultivating the skill (or superpower) of asking meaningful questions.

Fortunately, asking good questions is like writing as a skill: the more you practice, the better you get at it, and (according to Stephen King) you don't have to be an expert to do something worthwhile! The old adage that "there are no silly questions" still holds true. Of course, not every question prompts an insightful answer, but asking questions consciously and with clear objectives in mind can go a long way, especially in data work.

It is the hope of the author that this book has, at the very least, made you think about the topic and ponder on data's usefulness, both to you as an individual and to your organization. Happy questioning and answer-seeking!

Classic questions to ask yourself regarding data

"Questions are the beginning of wisdom."

Socrates

Question	Rationale
1. What is the purpose of the data?	Clarify why you're collecting and analyzing data. Is it for decision making, customer insights, or process improvement?
2. What is the scope of the data?	Determine what aspects of your business or organization the data represents (e.g., customers, employees, products).
3. How will we measure success?	Define key performance indicators (KPIs) and metrics to track progress and evaluate the effectiveness of data-driven initiatives.
4. Who has access to the data?	Establish clear roles and responsibilities for data ownership, accessibility, and security.
5. What are the potential biases in the data?	Consider factors like sampling errors, incomplete datasets, or biased assumptions that might impact analysis and decision making.

Question	Rationale
6. How will we integrate data from various sources?	Develop strategies for combining data from different systems, teams, or stakeholders to gain a more comprehensive view.
7. What are the ethical considerations?	Ensure compliance with regulations like GDPR, HIPAA, or CCPA, and consider the ethical implications of data-driven decisions on employees, customers, or any other stakeholders.
8. How will we maintain data quality and integrity?	Establish processes for data validation, cleansing, and backup procedures to ensure accuracy and availability.
9. What are the potential risks and consequences?	Identify potential downsides of relying too heavily on data-driven decisions, such as over-reliance or misinterpreting results.
10. How will we continuously improve and refine our approach?	Plan for ongoing evaluation, refinement, and iteration to ensure your data-driven initiatives remain effective and aligned with business objectives.
11. What are the low-hanging fruits when it comes to data projects?	Not all data products/projects are created equal. It is best to prioritize to maximize our ROI and minimize our risk.
12. What does success look like in a data project?	Beyond the metrics described in Q3, it would be good to have a clear idea of what a successful data project looks like when reporting its progress to the stakeholders.
13. What are the most pressing data-related challenges facing our organization/team right now, and how do we prioritize addressing them?	Similar to Q11, here we look at all the different challenges we face. Assessing them and ranking them is the next logical step, before coming up with a plan to tackle them.
14. What role does machine learning/deep learning play in our data initiative, and how do we integrate it with traditional data analysis methods?	Although both ML and DL are great methodologies, we need to take a step back and examine if they are right for us and how they could co-exist with other, less sophisticated methods we may be using.

Question	Rationale
15. How can we effectively communicate complex data insights to non-technical stakeholders, such as business leaders or clinicians?	Even if we understand data, it doesn't mean that the non-technical stakeholders do too (even though they might). Communicating our findings to them is key to ensuring progress with our data projects, and synergy.
16. What are the most promising data-driven opportunities for driving business value or improving outcomes in our organization, and how do we prioritize them?	Similarly to Q13, we should also look at opportunities related to data. Note that many of them may involve data we don't have (yet).
17. How do we balance the need for data governance and standardization with the need for flexibility and innovation in our data initiatives?	Data governance enables us to access the data swiftly and with minimal risk of errors. However, we also need to be flexible and not end up working for the data structures (it should be the other way around). Balancing these will require input from various people.
18. What are the key considerations when selecting a data visualization tool or platform, and what are some best practices for creating effective visualizations?	Although, in most cases, this is entirely unnecessary, sometimes we may need automated reporting and fancy graphics that specialized software offers. Who is going to consume these graphics/dashboards? Is it worth it for us to have a subscription fee to support that?
19. How can we leverage data storytelling techniques to make complex data insights more engaging and memorable for our audiences?	Everyone loves stories and if data is our game, we need to have data storytelling. Without a good story to convey our insights, challenges, and next steps, it would be hard to convince anyone of why what we are doing is worth the trouble.
20. What role do natural language processing (NLP) and text analytics play in our data initiative, and how do we apply them to extract insights from unstructured data?	Although this may appear anachronistic in the era of large language models (LLMs) like Llama, Minstrel, etc., it's something to consider. Perhaps one such LLM can be integrated too in this kind of data project.

Question	Rationale
21. How do we ensure that our data initiatives are transparent, accountable, and equitable, and what are some best practices for building trust with stakeholders around data-driven decision making?	High-level questions like this are also important, especially when liaising with senior management, CIOs, and even high-level consultants. However, be prepared for an equally high-level answer and for the need for follow-up questions to drill deeper into the topic.

Questions flowchart

"Questions are the engines of intellect – the cerebral machines that convert energy into motion."

David Hackett Fischer

The questions flowchart is a proposed workflow for developing and leveraging questions, ideally good ones, to tackle specific pain points, such as those discussed in the book (Figure B.1). It's not set in stone and it's not to be taken as gospel. You can think of it as a heuristic of sorts to help you develop your own system for tackling your organization's pain points methodically, leveraging data-related questions and the information you acquire through them.

Note that it's very important to take time to prepare before setting off on your questioning spree! Asking a good question isn't as simple as it sounds, plus the old adage that there are not any stupid questions doesn't mean that every question is going to be beneficial. Sure, you have to have the courage to ask any question that you feel a genuine curiosity to pursue the answer of, but if you are going to make the most of your time (as well as the time for the person you ask), it's good to make sure your questions are going to yield as much useful information as possible. This doesn't mean that it needs to be a lot of information, but enough to guide you towards the solution to your problem and possibly even improve your perspective in that area of concern.

It goes without saying that any question or series of questions you come up with needs to be accompanied by some research and a clear idea of what you are looking for. Unless you are clear on that latter part, it's unlikely you are going to get the most of the answers you obtain, even if they are genuinely good.

If this whole workflow reminds you of something, it's because it's inspired by scientific principles and methods for tackling research problems. However, it's not academic and not geared towards getting a publication out there. On the contrary, it is designed to be as practical as possible and drive action, once you have sufficient (actionable) information. It's important to remember that the responsibility of all this information lies with you, as what you do with the information you acquire is as important (if not more important) than the information itself.

Although it's not mentioned in the flowchart, it's always good to pause after getting an answer to each one of your questions. This gives you the mental space to process the new information, examine how it relates to the problem at hand, and potentially come up with good follow-up questions, if needed. This pause can therefore be as important as the question itself.

Finally, it's good to remember that the qualities you develop from leveraging such as framework, namely curiosity, interest, and open-mindedness, are crucial for any kind of problem-solving endeavor. Even if you forget or misplace the answers you've received from your questions, having these qualities will enable you to get new ones. So, developing your mindset through such upgrades can be more important than the information you acquire from your questioning process. In any case, such qualities are bound to develop organically when using this framework, as long as you are open to it and try to go beyond the words that are being exchanged.

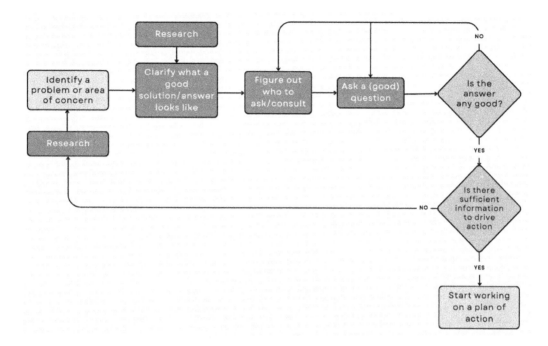

Figure B.1: Proposed flowchart for developing and leveraging (good) questions to tackle a given pain point.

Index